Solent Days and Ways

SUSANNAH RITCHIE

GW00634495

Printed by Conifer Press, Fareham, Hampshire

Published by Ensign Publications
2 Redcar Street, Shirley, Southampton SO1 5LL

First impression 1988

ISBN 185455 004 7

SOLENT DAYS AND WAYS
by
Susannah Ritchie

CONTENTS

Due acknowledgement is made to the proprietors of Hampshire *magazine for their kind permission to include, in the section on Cowes, a portion which appeared in their magazine in February 1971.*

The reviewers of the *Hamble River* book, published in 1984, were very kind. Some of them even asked for more. "What about a full length book?" wrote Rodger Witt rounding off his commentary in *Practical Boat Owner*. It seemed to me, after my exhausting toil, that seventy pages was quite adequate, but this is an attempt to provide a second instalment—including the publisher's suggestion that the area be widened to include the Solent.

Apparently Mr. Witt remembered the old office on a barge in Deacons Boatyard at Bursledon. He said he had often "clogged up the works" there—and so did a great many other people over the years. They came in winter for a warm by the stove, and in summer to gaze from the large upper deck windows at the passing craft. Sometimes they witnessed scenes of high drama. The ebb and flow of the water through Bursledon Bridge is constricted, and particularly on spring tides there is a very strong current. Strangers—rowing with all their strength in midstream, and making no progress—would have been carried along almost without effort had they come up-river in the eddy under the west bank. But the most spectacular were those who because of engine failure at a critical moment, or from inadequate power, had their yachts swept towards the bridge before the fascinated gaze of the onlookers.

The yard bo'sun was usually quick off the jetty with the *Mumford*, a 30ft. launch with a large fender on the high bow—and so to the rescue. The alternative for unhappy owners was that they were brought up abruptly by their mast hitting the bridge; sometimes it snapped, sometimes it held them. I did see one motor cruiser have its deckhouse top sliced off—a sensation for the skipper which must have resembled that experienced by the driver of a double-decker 'bus going through an arch which he is accustomed to negotiate with a single-decker.

The boatyard had very small beginnings after the 1914/18 War. Francis Deacon had been brought up at Reading and spent much of his early leisure on the Thames. He served in the Berkshire Yeo-manry and later in the R.A.S.C. and 1918 found him as a patient in the Royal Victoria Hospital at Netley. On being discharged he looked around for something to do, in the locality. In the course of some second-hand car dealing he met my father, and sold him an old single-cylinder De Dion. At that time cars were scarce, and very individual, nothing having been manufactured during the war except army vehicles. He also sold a Wolseley Stellite to one of my Island aunts, and taught her to drive. There were no driving tests in those days—there was hardly any traffic, and if you could keep the engine running and cope with the gear changing you were on the road. The De Dion was terribly noisy and extremely temperamental—and the starting handle was at the side, which at least prevented you from being run over if it started in a hurry, and in gear. . . . I remember that it stalled in front of a tram in Gosport one day, and in our haste to get away we left the handle on the kerb, but fortunately were alerted to this in time, by a spectator.

Another enthusiast who joined in some of these expeditions was a friend named Roberts, who then lived at Netley in a house named Ingleside, which is now the site of a housing development.

The second car which Francis found for my father was a two-cylinder Coventry Premier two-seater (with a front seat wide enough for three people), which the previous owner, Captain A.R.T. Kirby had named "The Mousetrap" because of its flat appearance. It did very well—the only slight mishap was that one end of the silencer came adrift in Northam, near the T.V.S. Studio, and we rattled over the tram setts with a tremendous din.

I had forgotten all about Capt. Kirby until I saw in the November 1984 *Hampshire* magazine a photograph of a little schooner, the *Mynonie R. Kirby* which had been named after his young daughter. The ship was originally the *Cadwallader Jones*, and I gather from the article is now no more.

My father eventually found a piece of land for sale on the west bank of the Hamble River, near Bursledon Bridge and below the railway station, and here Francis started his business, with one small shed, the first job being the repair of an outboard motor for Squadron Leader A.F. Somerset-Leeke. His connection with the river went back to his childhood on his father's steam yacht, which appears in some of the early photographs of Bursledon Pool. He remained a customer at the yard for the rest of his life, and many people will remember his yacht *Glenshane* which cruised extensively. He told me that as a boy on holiday he would be sent ashore to get milk from Hackett's farmhouse in Old Bursledon (now Lattice Cottage).

The Deacons at Upcott. 1932.

Francis Deacon married a V.A.D. whom he met at Netley Hospital and they lived at first on an ex-M.L. *Mayfly* at the yard. As mentioned in the *Hamble River* book, Primmer & Snook had already established themselves on the site nearest to the bridge, very good relations were built up with them, and continued throughout the years until Mr. Primmer died and after a while Mr. Snook retired. In a later ownership the two yards were merged.

After the 1914/18 War a little group of ex-servicemen founded the Navigators & General Insurance Company. A few of them lived on houseboats, and consequently knew more than most about the perils of marine insurance. Their illustrated handbook was a gem – really funny. One of the Navigators, Richard Faulkner, who was hoping to get married (and live on a boat . . .) asked Mrs. Deacon if he might bring his "intended" to tea, and he besought Mrs. Deacon to play down such trifling drawbacks as drip tins which hung from the saloon bulkheads and were liable to tip their contents over anyone tall enough to collide with them. All went well – and the marriage duly took place.

(Capt. Richard W.A. Faulkner, who died in 1950, was in command of the Clacton Lifeboat during the evacuation from Dunkirk).

Francis was a large cheerful man who never worried about trifles, and the customers liked him. He usually wore dilapidated grey flannels, a woollen cardigan, and smoked a disreputable pipe. He chose his spectacles at Woolworths – where most things were still sixpence – old money. People didn't really notice what he wore, his personality took precedence over his appearance, and anyway most boat people don't dress up. They come to the water to get away from all that. Some of our owners in very scruffy clothes were celebrities escaping from their existence.

His activities often involved some little job necessitating a soldering iron being poked into the office stove to heat, or pieces of wire being deflexed with a penknife. Some time later when they lived at

Upcott, the seventeenth century house overlooking the river, he fitted a copper pipe which came up from the cellars through the floor by the sittingroom hearth, to give draught to the fire. We teased him about it at the time, but it was quite an idea, subsequently patented by someone else.

The travellers of those days included an old friend from Caversham, A.T.M. Ayling, a delightful character who was with Stuart Turner of Henley-on-Thames for thirty years. A large proportion of small yachts had Stuart Turner engines as auxiliary power, they were very trouble-free and it was easy to get spares. Mr. Ayling made regular calls on all the yards, and in fact when petrol was rationed in the 1939/45 War he did some of his rounds on horseback, being devoted to both varieties of horse power.

Montagu Smith, who started the firm of wholesale marine distributors now in St. Michael's Square at Southampton, had a store in those days facing the Town Quay. He was a large jovial man who drove around in an open Bean car, from which he seemed to overflow.

There were many paint travellers—it was a job which I suppose most ex-naval people considered they were particularly fitted to do, and we had all sorts, from ex-Admirals downwards.

By the beginning of the thirties Francis had bought the barge/houseboat which served as an office, and had gone to live at Upcott on Station Hill, formerly owned by the Ewer family, John Iremonger Eckless, (see previous book), and more recently the station master's house. The name of the last name of the station master at Bursledon was Tarrant—and by a strange coincidence (I assume the B.B.C. producers did not know it), the name of the village in the serial "Howard's Way", was given as Tarrant. As the film people changed the name-boards at the station while they were on location, passengers were in some doubt as to whether they were arriving at Bursledon, or not.

By 1934 the office work was getting out of hand, and it was sug-

Deacons Yard in the Thirties.

gested that I should come home (after seven years with Thomas Cook & Son) and deal with matters—which proved to be helpful when the war came along and practically everything which was needed for the contracts had to be applied for on multitudes of forms. I began by trying to tidy up the place, but—to go all nautical—the tide was against me, and so was the solid presence of many awkwardly shaped objects with which the office was cluttered. Francis had collected a circle of friends and acquaintances who delighted to get to the yard and discuss with him all those topics which boat owners find endlessly fascinating. Nowadays waterside cafes are decorated with nets and floats and suchlike objects. Without effort the office had become littered with pieces of ironmongery, anchors, blocks, and items for repair or resale brought in by customers. The walls were hung with shackles on strings, and decorated with the half-models of old boats, and it was a constant struggle to keep the working area clear. Sails were a particular nuisance—in those days many were still of heavy canvas and difficult to move, unlike the modern terylene—and they were put into a railed-off section of floor which was a trapdoor to "down below". But usually they overflowed this pen while waiting for sail-makers' attention.

A shattering occasion was when I tipped some rubbish from a miniature chest of drawers into the office stove. All the mica blew out with a series of bangs, there being some tiny cartridges amongst the junk.

An important piece of equipment—and even then an antique—was a Remington typewriter which must have been one of the earliest models. As a fast touch-typist of considerable strength I could produce a machine-gun noise which drove all but the really persist-

A Renner Lift — at Moodys Swanwick Yard.   Photo J.B. Heynes

ent from the cabin. Francis Deacon would beg me to leave the typing until he went out into the yard to look at jobs—and the obvious remedy— to buy a modern machine—never even occurred to him.

Outside, the boatsheds were of the same primitive pattern—poles were driven into the soft mud, with iron sheets for roofing, and most of these shelters were open on the river side. (see two old photographs). Nearly all the yachts were of wooden construction then, and were hauled out of the water under cover for the winter, advantage being taken of high tides, plus cradles, planks well daubed with slipway grease, and much manual labour. The Renner Lifts which nowadays move yachts with ease anywhere on a good hard level surface, were dreams of the future.

There were no pile moorings in the early days—ground tackle was laid, anchors and heavy chain, and owners who "sailed" on their moorings were very unpopular, because they dragged the underwater gear out of position. The dockyard sales provided some of this material, and were attended by the boatyard people who also bought small ex-service craft there too. At them Francis met Fred Watts of Gosport and the Pounds of Portchester and other interested parties.

Two regular winter visitors who came in for a warm by the stove were Wilfrid and Eric Humphrey from Lands End House, which in those days had no central heating, and, facing north, was extremely cold. Wilfrid usually kept his coat collar turned up and a cap pulled well down . They owned the German built motor yacht *Kestrel*, and were very inventive engineers. Sometimes they ran around on the river in a boat pushed by the jet from a fire hose. . . .After the mention of Eric in the *Hamble River* book I had a telephone call from someone who had bought *Kestrel* after finding her sunk in Shoreham harbour. He had her surveyed, and said that the hull was quite sound, and he was going ahead with reconditioning. I found him a photograph of the boat when she was lying off Lands End House years before, which was useful for comparison.

Another person who spent a good deal of time in the office was Arthur Leney, a judge of champion pigs at the big shows. He was a man who always looked on the black side, and in the late thirties was full of doom and gloom about the approaching war. He ruined my early mornings at the office for a long time. He had a large yacht, *Herga*, on our moorings, and drove a Rolls-Royce. Later he went down river to live at "Otterholme" which is a house with a splendid site by the water, on the east below Universal Shipyard. He made a lovely iris garden there. Since his day the house has been altered and enlarged considerably. We also converted an ex-Admiralty harbour launch for him. It was very smart, painted green, with a brass funnel, and he named it *Mosquito*. The charm of these little steam engined craft is that they run so silently. We overhauled lots of them during the war, when Frank Paton-Moore was our expert.

"Mosquito" a 48 ft. ex-Admiralty Steam Launch.

One of the long-standing customers of the yard was R.A. Calvert, who is mentioned briefly in the *Hamble River* book as one of the Cierva team who worked on the invention of the Autogiro, forerunner of the Helicopter, Sea Scout master at Hamble in the twenties, and hi-jacked from Grenada in 1980 and presumably murdered, his little yacht being found holed and stripped of all her gear on the shores of St. Lucia.

My father met him in about 1920 when a field full of seaplanes was being offered for sale at Lee-on-Solent Air Station. Sir Mansfield Cumming (who had been my father's C.O. in the Boom Defence in pre-war days, and Captain "C" of the British Secret Service during the 1914/18 War), bought a great many of them and they were towed to Bursledon by a Lancia lorry at the rate of two a day, throwing up a great cloud of white dust en route, since the roads then were not surfaced with tarmacadam. They were parked in a field at Bursledon Lodge, and re-sold very cheaply at £5 apiece. The hulls had a tunnel through them which took an axle with two wheels, and as far as I can remember they were towed tail first. As flying boats the hulls were of wood, and by cutting off the tail section and putting in a transom, plus an outboard engine, there was a motor boat without too much trouble. My childhood memory of them was that the cabin had a peculiar smell from varnish or dope which had been used, and the sliding hatch seemed all too likely to jam if the machine landed badly. I didn't like the thought.

Reg Calvert came along and bought one to convert, and my father later introduced him to Francis Deacon, after which he kept various boats at the yard. Reg worked as a draughtsman with Pemberton Billing, at Supermarine, and at Avro, and always said that the most significant period of his working life was when Don Juan de la Cierva came to Hamble for his invention the Autogiro to be built there. In a letter Reg wrote "I was responsible under him for all the early project work on these craft, and I feel it is an honour to be able to say that I was the first draughtsman in this world to work

Six-metre under repair. 1935.

how much they owe to Cierva, for it was his early work on the Autogiro which made the helicopter possible".

Reg Calvert was an enthusiastic traveller—for which he took time off from his job—and always found it easy to get another one on his return. The 1939/45 War anchored him to desk work in Yeovil and Cheltenham (not his scene at all . . .) so by the time peace came he was full of ideas for a new life. He had previously visited the West Indies, which he considered to have the best climate for his ideal existence, but travel between the islands was difficult. So on a beach in Barbados, with local labour, he built a little yacht, *Carib*, to his own design, shipping out a Stuart Turner engine and sundry gear from England. This 5 tonner cost him £800 and was his home and his means of transport for many years. It enabled him to visit all the small islands, Bequia being one of his particular favourites.

To begin with he came back to England from May to September, but after the death of his mother who lived in Southampton he remained in the West Indies permanently, and in later years was based at St. George's harbour in Grenada.

In the period while he was commuting by the French Line to and from Southampton, we had two of his little yachts, *Rona II* and *Seal* at the boatyard, and I made charter bookings for them for the summer, when Reg was supposed to be in England to see the hirers in and out each Saturday. The regular people who had the boats each year were not any problem, but when Reg was delayed in his return, and we had parties who rang up on Saturday to say that unfortunately (for us) they had left the boat at some other harbour and would we collect it—then we tore our hair and wished Reg and his charters somewhere. . . . The next party would be hanging about, and someone had to check the engine, refuel it, change the gas bottle, and clean up, as soon as we zoomed into the jetty with the abandoned yacht in tow. We were not amused.

We had a few owners who took people across Channel and to Guernsey and Jersey, but even though in charge of their own ships

on a rotating wing aircraft capable of cross-country flight. I wonder how many of those who have been rescued by helicopters realise they were not always happy about it. With paying passengers they felt obliged to "go places" when conditions were not what they would have chosen.

Reg had many happy years in the West Indies, and one of our souvenirs is the photograph showing how he thought the Hamble River could be "improved", with a few palm trees, a coral beach, and the right temperature of course.

Gone are the days when it was safe to leave dinghies, oars, and other items lying about. Most boat owners are honest people but it is impossible to shut a boatyard with customers coming and going all the time, and now there is a great deal of organised thieving. Inflatables, outboard motors, and all the expensive navigational gear is very likely to be stolen, even if padlocked and chained. Boats on trailers disappear, trailer and all, in fact that probably makes the job easier. With thousands of craft in a river like the Hamble it is quite impossible for the river police to prevent this—and in addition there is a constant alert for drug smugglers.

In the "Lost" category we found that owners transferring gear from cars to their dinghies tended to leave things lying on the jetties. Many items were found and handed into the office and later claimed. One lady had cause for rejoicing—she lost a handbag containing her chequebook, credit cards, keys, and quite a large sum of money, while transporting gear from car to boat. On a hard down-river another customer of the yard was attending to his craft, with his two young sons, when they saw something floating by. The boys dashed out in their dinghy and retrieved it, discovering a handbag (plastic) in good seaworthy condition, on course for the Solent. So it was returned to the owner with the contents dry and intact, after she had spent some time in frantic search.

Two large vessels which gave the yard employment in the early days were first an old coaster named *Pioneer* which was aground in Fareham Creek, and was brought round to Bursledon and converted into a houseboat. The second was an off service ferry, the *Lymington*, a paddler, which had a great deal of space in the passenger accommodation and made a luxurious houseboat. These were both for the same owner, who lived on them in turn, and subsequently bought an island in a Scottish loch and lived there in solitary state with his Man Friday. All their supplies had to be collected from the nearest town by boat, and in bad weather it sounded anything but an ideal arrangement. From his dictatorial manner I suspected that he had been a schoolmaster at some time, which was somehow borne out by the fact that when living on the island he would post Francis copies of books by one of the most widely read authors of the time—with all the split infinitives corrected and critical notes in the margins. ... .

It is said that if you call "Mac" down an engineroom hatch anywhere in the world, a Scot will answer you, and our boatyard attracted a good many throughout the years.

One in particular was on the staff for a long time, during which I heard many stories. He had been brought up in Argyllshire in the late eighteen hundreds. In those days the maintenance of roads in Scotland was done by private contractors, of whom Mac's father was one. For this work he bought fairly large quantities of gunpowder—for blasting operations, and on the principle of "keeping your powder dry" it was stored under a bed in a spare room. This caused a sleepless night for a certain Uncle Duncan, who arrived for a night's accommodation and was warned that on no account must he strike matches. ....

The description of the household shopping expeditions was of a marathon. Mac was first allowed to accompany his mother when he was about six years old. They awoke about half past three, dressed, breakfasted, and set off in darkness. They walked down the glen to Dunoon where they caught a steamer and arrived in Glasgow about nine o'clock. His mother went to her usual suppliers and ordered flour by the sack, and other goods in sufficient quantities to last them for some time, and this provision was all shipped later to Dunoon to wait for a farmcart going up the glen.

Anything wanted urgently they had to carry with them. He said that on one occasion his mother carried a lamp and he was entrusted with the shade, for that long and tiring journey homewards, and there was great rejoicing when they arrived with it unbroken, after an eleven mile walk on a rough track at the end of that very long day. Little wonder that the Scots made good under tough conditions in distant countries.

Living so far from civilization made quite a problem of the children's education, but Mac's father solved this by giving a home to a University man whose family were anxious to keep him away from the temptation of heavy drinking, and this exile was a tutor to the three young ones. Life in the glen taught them much lore—for example, that the Highland cattle, such quiet creatures in spite of their shaggy and fearsome appearance, would come down from the hills well in advance of bad weather, as they sensed its approach. The sheep farmers would have a few goats with the hill flock, to eat the tempting grass and herbage on dangerous ledges, so that the sheep would not return. A goat can get into very tight corners and leap back to safety.

Mac went to sea at an early age, and knocked about the world, acquiring much experience and a wide outlook, which, retailed with truly Scottish humour, made him a most entertaining companion. My father visited him when he was temporarily housebound with some slight illness, and after that he was a frequent visitor to us and I listened in to many tales that were told.

The behaviour of the accountant auditors who visited us to check the boatyard books always caused us some amusement. The first audit after my arrival was undertaken by a family firm, with father and sons all being equally boat-minded people. Papa began the check, leaving eldest son to continue—but eldest son was so enraptured with the view from our barge/office windows that he would sit

Boatyard flooded at High Spring tides.

for hours with a book open before him, intent on all the goings on outside. He would gladly have stayed for weeks . . . and only after anxious nudgings from Francis Deacon was he recalled to base.

Later auditors, from city firms, arrived on the first morning in dark suits with highly polished shoes, and briefcases. A space was cleared for them, with difficulty, but they were gradually indoctrinated into life on the shoreline. For instance, I kept a dinghy tied to the rails, so that if the tide came exceptionally high I could row along the length of the drive to the main road, to get home to lunch. They thought it was a huge joke, but by the end of their first week they had got the message, appeared in roll-neck sweaters and rubber boots! There was an eagerness to come again next year—which we found most gratifying in view of the spartan conditions prevailing.

These conditions were hard on some of the girls who came to work in the office in following ownerships. Mrs Sheridan engaged one who came the first day in a spotless outfit, and for lack of space (we were changing from the original barge office to the Log Cabin) was parked temporarily with her ledgers at the top of stairs leading to "down below" on the Sheridan's houseboat. Imagine the poor girl's horror when, having all her books spread about, open—down rushed a horde of muddy King Charles Cavaliers, leaving pawmarks on everything including her own clothes. To her great credit she stuck it out, ending up buying two of the puppies whom she loved dearly. New puppies were named after the yachts, and for twelve years I had the great company of Gypsy Moth. The dogs shared a very large wooden bed in the main office, and one day when most of them had gone to a show, some visitors gazed fearfully at this affair and remarked "You must have a very large dog" . . .

Lavinia Sheridan has always been a remarkable woman— energetic, enthusiastic, and ready to accept any new challenge. She described herself as "a Puddletown girl"—actually she lived at Waterston which is the house nearby, which Thomas Hardy chose as the setting for Bathsheba Everdene in *Far From the Madding Crowd*. Here Lavinia gardened, a pastime which gave her pleasure wherever she found herself subsequently. She married H.L. Brinsley-Sheridan, a descendent of the famous dramatist, and their elder son is another Richard Brinsley-Sheridan. They lived in London, but when the four children came to Hamble River to sail Optimist dinghies Lavinia discovered Deacons Boatyard for sale, and promptly bought it. She did a great deal of reorganising, and with Ron Packman as her shipwright foreman the yard built a number of yachts to designs of Fred Parker, James McGruer and others. One yacht *Marelle* was for Mrs Honor-Spink, who was an outstanding member of the sailing fraternity at that time.

The children grew up and married, Lavinia moved to a farm in Dorset for a while, and then to a remote valley in Wales. The last move was to be near her sister, and since living there she has cultivated her talent as an artist, and exhibited her paintings at London galleries.

When she came to Bursledon she had ten Cavalier King Charles spaniels, the dogs which appear in Royal paintings and tapestries far earlier than King Charles II. In Victorian times this breed had degenerated into lapdogs with short legs and pug noses, but in 1926, thanks to an American, Mr Roswell Eldridge, who offered prizes at Crufts for five years in succession, for the Cavalier in its rightful form, they are now back to the sporting type with long faces and flat skulls, able to enjoy out of door activites. The most beautiful of the Sheridan pack was Louise, a tri-colour which Carol Sheridan had found tied up in the backyard when they lived in London, and had rescued. Louise knew that she was special, she sat up straight, with her long ears dangling, and looked down her aristocratic nose. "Venture", who lived at the yard with Jack and Dorrie Palmer, who renamed him "Fred" because of his likeness in character to the cartoon dog—had much the same idea. One day, when a man passing through the yard spoke to him, Fred eyed him with displeasure, turned and walked away. "Well" said the man, "it's the first time I've been snubbed by a dog". "Happy" and "Lucky" were always known as the "Maiden Aunts", and there was "Chanticler" who belonged to Lavinia's mother Mrs Rawlence. He was always beautifully groomed, and regarded his boisterous (and often muddy) cousins with distrust and some apprehension when he visited the yard. They were a most interesting and lovable little bunch, and many people fell for their charms, including the actress Susannah York who had a yacht with us then.

The job-sheets which were issued gave us daily exercise, as some of the apprentice boys, ideas of spelling were phonetic, in "English as she is spoke", and we became accustomed to "cork" for "caulk",

A pre-1914 River Launch "Medina" in creek on Salterns Marsh, — it looks very dated now, but much used for picnics then.

etc., but the main trouble was that we always seemed to have several yachts with very similar names. At one time we had *Ruana*, *Roande*, and *Ruanda*, and pairs such as *Maresca* and *Marishka*, which left the chaps scratching their heads and licking their pencils tryng to sort them out.

We were very interested when the yard was building a range of 33ft centreboard yachts, and there was a prospective buyer whose purchase depended on the sale of a famous painting which he owned. It was of an Indian holding some Cheetahs on a leash, and was auctioned at one of the London salerooms, realising the amount of money needed to finance the purchase of the boat, which was in due course named *Cheetah*.

In the twenties and thirties most yachts were of wood, and built individually, which made them more interesting, and recognisable, than the modern moulded hulls. One particular beauty which has been on the Hamble for years in one ownership is Johnny Johnson's *Escape* a Colin Archer yacht, now in the Swanwick Marina. The owners have lived aboard for a very long time, and their two sons were brought up afloat. The younger one, Paul, who was working in the Shetlands in the late fifties, sailed home to Bursledon across the North Sea in an 18ft Shetland fishing boat *Venus* in 1961, and subsequently made other long single handed voyages.

Another lovely yacht was *Tuloa*, a 33ft Auxiliary Bermudan Sloop designed by James McGruer. The couple who owned her in those days prided themselves on sailing her, without any assistance from the moorings at Bursledon into the Solent, and back again, on each occasion when they took her out.

Dutch boats were a joy, and of infinite variety. We had a small one at the yard, *Moeder De Gans*, (Mother Goose), 30ft long OA, 24ft on the waterline, and countless people pleaded with the owner, a Capt. Shand, to sell it to them. There were blue and white tiles around the interior of the main cabin, and the tiller was carved as a goose. Later a few wooden hulls were imported from Holland, but when completed they lacked the detail of the boats which had been used over there, which had decorations akin to our Narrow Boats on the canals, and to the old style Romany caravans—loving details added by the people who lived in them.

An old copy of Lloyds Register of Yachts would be a good choice of a Desert Island book for me, because it would bring back many memories of yachts and their owners.

In my early days at the boatyard the *Dulcibella* was still lying in a mudberth on the east bank of the river, and was regarded by me with great interest because *The Riddle of Sands* by Erskine Childers was one of the favourite books of my childhood. I read it many times. I see from reviews that Mr Maldwin Drummond has now written *The Riddle*—a history of the *Dulcibella*, and it mentions Mr

Edwards who bought the boat from Moodys Yard for £12. Mr. Edward's granddaughter, now ninety-seven tells me that she remembers the deckhouse structure which he built, and in which she often had tea with him. She also recalled being stung by a wasp which crawled up her leg while she was aboard—and being too embarrassed to mention it.

Amongst our owners we had two very decorative people, who stood out from the rest because they obviously did not work on their cruiser, but could have gone on the stage in one of the Novello shows at a moment's notice. Inevitably they were known as "The Dancing Years".

We also had a lady, much photographed for the *Tatler* and glossy magazines. She and her husband had a small auxiliary cutter to which they came at intervals. One morning Alf Foulkes went out to do a little job aboard—and either the yacht's dinghy was on the other side, or the lady's husband had gone ashore in it—but as Alf was about to make fast his painter, over the edge of the hatch of the apparently unoccupied yacht came a hand, dripping blood . . . "Cor, it gave me a turn" he said afterwards—and that was his introduction to coloured nail varnish. For some years we looked after a sailing scow for Winchester College. The boys who used it came by train, involving a change at St. Denys. Mrs. Deacon frequently had to dry their clothes before they were in a fit state to make the return journey, and in the meantime the owners hung about in borrowed garments several sizes too large—they always seemed to be rather thin little boys.

Somewhat of a contrast was the Royal Artillery Yacht Club, for whom we kept two yachts in Mrs Sheridan's time. These were sailed by a Brigadier and a whole gang of Majors. The latter were young, and usually arrived on a Friday afternoon, disrupting our office and causing the King Charles spaniels to open their eyes wide at the disturbance of their rest. It was wages day, and we tried hard to get everything worked out and the cash in the envelopes before

the Larkhill crowd arrived, since we could rarely get anything done while they were around. They were like boys let out of school, full of jokes and joy at the prospect of a weekend afloat.

On another Friday afternoon, but in the winter, two of us were in the office when we were startled by a loud bang and a red glow beneath us. Dorrie Palmer, who dealt with the wages, flew to the safe for the money, and I gathered up the sleepy King Charles's and urged them down the outer staircase—they not very pleased at being out in the cold. Fortunately it was not too serious—an oxy-acetylene cylinder had exploded, and beyond that there was no damage, but it was quite a fright. I never liked being upstairs in the log cabin building, (so-called because the exterior was encased in bark). In fact nothing was so good as our old Barge Houseboat office which we had in the beginning. Latterly the offices were in buildings almost at water level, in the part of the yard which had formerly belonged to Primmer & Snook, and when there were high tides with a gale behind them we had to be ready to get out quickly, having lifted everything off the floors. If the tide came at night, unexpectedly, we would find everything awash in the morning, and live damply for the next few days. Periodically the buildings were "jacked up" by Eddy White and his assistants, but it was never enough to cope with freak tides.

Our other club boat was interesting—*Overlord* the ex-German yacht of the Hitler regime—built in 1936, and after the war bought by the Offshore Cruising Club.

A colourful character on the board of directors of Deacons Boatyard Ltd., in the seventies was the internationally known Yacht Designer Angus Primrose.

On Regatta days Angus entered whole-heartedly into the spirit of the thing, taking part in most of the afternoon events and falling into the water when he thought it would add to the fun. Admittedly Francis Deacon didn't go to such lengths, but he directed proceedings through a loud-hailer and came home hoarse by evening, hav-

The late Colonel H.M.E. Bradshaw (centre) with the Regatta Sailing Committee on the pier at Warsash.
Mrs. K. Robinson (time-keeper) stands beside him.

ing enjoyed the affair tremendously. He had the traditions of Henley and the Thames from his young days, while Angus had lived at St. Mawes as a boy, so they were both well versed in aquatics.

When the Regatta restarted after the war the handicapping for the sailing was done by Lt. Colonel H.M.E. Bradshaw, who ran the Warsash Yacht Agency from a boat hauled up on the hard opposite the Rising Sun. He was a very large ginger-haired man, 6ft.5in., with a powerful voice and a splendid record. Appropriately his first name was Hercules, but he was known as "Monty". Born in 1897 he joined the Hampshire Regiment at the outbreak of the first war, and won the M.C. in France when he was only a little over seventeen years of age. After a varied career—with the Lothian and Border Horse as adjutant, with them crossing the Arabian Desert, and for two years wearing the silver greyhound badge of a King's Messenger, he retired in 1930, and then was much involved with yacht racing, being Hon. Secretary of the Solent Racing Association until illness forced him to retire in 1960. For thirteen years he held the record for the best time in the Round the Island Race, sailed in Mr Ronnie Burton's *Iskareen*, and he had many successes with his six metre *Zenith*. Altogether a very colourful character.

In those days we had the Regatta suppers at the Bold Forester, Sarisbury—the landlord, Mr Foreman, being on the Committee. Our most popular entertainer at these functions was the Southampton "Magic Circle" man Jeff Atkins, who later became very well known, sawing ladies in half and causing them to float in the air unsupported by any visible means.

Before the marinas provided so many berths for yachts it was an attractive proposition to buy any craft which had its own mooring afloat, so that the site could be used for say two or three boats. Owners were often quite desperate in their search for somewhere to tie up. However, I recall one instance where Francis turned down such an opportunity without hesitation, because it involved buying an unlucky ship. It was an old yacht with a pointed bow, and it had quite a record of tragedies. I can remember three of them. It may all have been coincidence, but you wonder. . . . I am convinced that houses have an atmosphere—either happy, from the people who have lived in them—or the reverse, and some I would not consider at all. Therefore a boat could absorb past tragedies too.

Long ago houseboats were regarded as delightful holiday places, and a vision was evoked of square flat-roofed wooden affairs on substantial barge foundations, moored to a river bank, and hung around with baskets of flowers.

The housing shortages after the two wars changed all that. The wooden M.L's of the Great War made very comfortable living quarters with the engines removed, and they lasted a long time and were not unsightly. One great advantage, in those pre-central-heating days was that a wooden ship, being waterproof as regards the hull, was also draught-proof and therefore very snug below. Deck leaks were a separate problem. In contrast, after the 1939/45 War another type of houseboat appeared, the ugly metal-plated box-like L.C.I's and L.C.T's. They were a great eyesore on our rivers, and inside was condensation. . . .

The drawback to all of them was that unless a berth was available alongside a jetty with a power cable for electricity and a pipeline for water, it was necessary to run a lighting set to charge batteries, and get the water tanks filled somehow. People who were on the Hamble in those days will remember Capt. Harry Smith, who patrolled in P.5 dispensing fuel, water, Calor Gas, and necessities. However, in a secluded berth you might be off their round, and in winter when the supply boat was overhauled you would be left high and (literally) dry. People with running water, in taps, h.&.c. do not realise what the lack of it can mean.

There was an old yacht named *Dawn* in a mudberth at the yard and one of the painters sojourned on it during the working week. It must have been bleak, but he preferred this to travelling to and from Gosport every day. Dodsworth was a dear, and always philosophical, even when *Dawn* lifted out of her berth on an unusually high tide, and didn't go back into her hole properly, causing him to live at an uncomfortable angle until the situation was righted.

It is generally accepted that sailing men are sentimental about their boats, to which they devote all their spare time and money and nothing, it must be admitted, costs more for upkeep than a boat. Men who make their living by fishing seem more inclined to regard the vessel as a necessary means to an end but not in every case. One of the saddest sights I have seen was of an ex-professional fisherman dragging himself about a mile to the shore, and leaning on a wall to look longingly down the estuary towards the sea. He did this every day until his illness made it impossible for him to walk. This man had owned a small boat for most of his life, and spent the main part of his time aboard. He had married a "land" family, but she remained in her original home looking after an elderly father and brother, so her husband had no real place of his own—except his boat. When ill-health compelled him to sell the craft because there was no-one to keep it pumped or see to it, it must have broken his heart. No more misty mornings in the Solent, or sunset evenings as he sailed out to the fishing grounds, his few possessions around him, his cooking utensils and enough for his simple needs. The boat was his life, and when it was gone his life was over.

Mr W.L. (Bill) Hobbs, retired Marine Surveyor, lives in Hamble at a house fittingly named "Becalmed". He was born at Netley, where his father had a printing business, but he went to Lukes Yard, Hamble, in 1923, aged fifteen, and was later apprenticed to boat-building. He has very happy memories of the Luke brothers who took a fatherly interest in all their employees, worked the same hours, and knew their families. They encouraged the young apprentices to go out sailing in the yachts, so that they would do a better job on them. This was a friendly yard, with the brothers often going back in the evenings to have a word with the owners and skippers. Mr Hobbs said that the first Luke yard was at Itchen Ferry in 1829, and later they were at Hamble Point. Several models of sea-planes were made there, but never progressed to the flying stage, which was a pity. Young Bill Hobbs later moved to the drawing office and with encouragement from Mr Luke gained a place at the University College for Naval Architects. When war came in 1939 and there were was not much to do, he transferred to the Warship Production design office at Thornycrofts, and by the end of the war was working for the Ministry of Labour instructing women and "dilutees" (his expression) in boatbuilding. He returned to Luke Bros. Yard, but when it was sold to Port Hamble Ltd., in 1954 he became a Lloyds Surveyor, and continued thus for twenty years, retiring in 1974

Mr Hobbs has a fund of stories about local characters—one "Jargie" Bedford, returning along the footpath from Netley to Hamble after a drinking session, wandered off course, and ended up asleep on a grave in the Military Cemetery of Netley Hospital, where he awoke in the morning to find "a ruddy great angel" hovering above him.

Along the lane from "Becalmed" is the Sail Loft where the late Mrs Williams carried on a sail-making business with her assistant Mr Young. Mr Young often called at Deacons to measure up, and he was a very quiet man, but of Mrs Williams, said Bill Hobbs, "How she could talk; she must have been vaccinated with a gramophone needle".

They seem to have been very good neighbours, in spite of the fact that she frequently left her car in the lane with no lights on. Coming home in the dark one evening he went in and told her that he had just "biffed" her car. When the lamentation died down he assured her that he had not really done so, but that someone would certainly damage themselves and it, if she did not mend her ways. When she retorted that it would run her battery down, he said that was remedied by buying a new battery, and was cheaper than buying a new car. I didn't gather whether they ever sorted this one out. . . .

Mrs Williams' daughter-in-law still runs the business of sail-making with Mr Young.

Surveyors always asked permission to inspect yachts in the variious yards before making their visits, and on one occasion Mr Hobbs recalled that a prospective buyer wished to look at a yacht, hauled out at Moodys Yard, on a Sunday, that being the only day on which he could attend. Mr Hobbs, bearing in mind that A.H. Moody (great-grandfather of the present generation) was a staunch chapel-goer, approached him with the proposal, and said that if he had any objection they would of course defer to his wishes in the matter. A.H. considered carefully, and then said gravely "I will leave a ladder for you".

The Hamble River Sailing Club fostered some first-class dinghy sailors over the years, amongst them John Oakeley and Dick Vine. In those days Dick's father owned the old "J" Class *Velsheda*, and the family lived aboard at Swanwick, Dick sailing his firefly *Elf II*. He won the North American Championship in 1957 and was in the International Team races in Toronto (where he now lives). In a recent letter he said "I don't sail anymore, too old and fat for dinghies. *Fireball* was my last boat. I fly gliders now, much less wet, and still do ice-boating in the cold weather here". He recalled some of the adventures with his friend Bob Gingell, who was an apprentice at Moodys Yard and son of the Sarisbury Green schoolmaster. Bob had a gaff rigged boat *Duck*, and Dick said "the corners of the transom were so bashed up that Bob cut off a foot and put a new transom in, so that there was good wood to drive the nails through. We were swamped in Fawley Creek at near low water by the wash from the Channel Islands Ferry (*Falaise*), broke the boom, and sailed loose-footed (footloose.!) to Lymington. We slept in an old barge with rats, and had breakfast at a cafe. Bob knocked his kipper off his plate onto the floor, picked it up, and slapped it back on the plate saying 'Now stay there you. . . .' By this time, we had the attention of all". . . . Those were the days evidently.

All the Hamble River Sailing Club youngsters owed a great deal to Nicholas Robinson who organised the weekly races, and most deservedly in 1958 won the Silk Cut Award for outstanding service in the Club Section. He joined in 1925 at the age of twelve, and has been secretary, vice-commodore, and commodore, devoting himself to the well-being of the Club for sixty years. He is reckoned to have started some 120,000 boats, and his services have been called for by Olympic training regattas, European and World Championships, and the London Boat Show. He initiated the Inshore Rescue Service, and has been ably supported by his wife Kippy.

Nicholas Robinson was born at Quay House, Hamble (now the Royal Southern Yacht Club), his father Gregory being a marine painter and naval historian, so he really belongs to the village. At

Dick Vine, — Champion dinghy sailing at Hamble about 1950, when his father owned "Velsheda", and they lived aboard at Swanwick.

their Studio in Satchell Lane the couple specialise in the printing of yachting programmes and sailing instructions, which they were the first to prepare on waterproof paper.

The mention by Dick Vine of the boys' boat being swamped by wash from the *Falaise*, reminded me that there was always a slight feeling between the officers of the old British Rail cross-Channel boats and the "yachties". The ferries had a "dim" view, literally, of the pinpoints on their radar screens which in many instances were inadequately lit private pleasure craft. As a part of the yachting business, and with an old friend on the *Falaise* for some time, I heard both sides of the story.

This particular officer, George Hunt, had spent some years in the South American passenger service from Southampton, and was an entertaining teller of tales of the sea. He had a distinguished war career, and an Irishman's sense of humour – one of his quirks being to fill in his place of birth, on official forms, as Dublin Zoo. . . . When queried by doubting Thomases, this turned out to be fact, his father having been the curator, and George and his brother being brought up amongst the lions and tigers.

The liners in and out of Southampton had their troubles too, for if they exceeded a certain speed the wash they made often sucked deckchairs off the Solent beaches, and the town councils at Ryde and Cowes and other places sent anguished protests to the shipping companies.

There is a wide difference between the ladies of the Elizabethan era who walked on the lawns of the Royal Yacht Squadron at Cowes in white or navy pleated skirts, and were transported in spotless launches without getting near anything wet or muddy and the sailing women now, who help with all the jobs, and contrive to look smart at the same time. In between these two types of jobs were some mannish yachtswomen of the thirties, who had boats of their own. One of these, whom we had at the yard for a time, smoked cigars and was nicknamed "Miss Daggers" by the men, because she wore a knife at her waistbelt. Another, who held a Yachtmaster's ticket, had an Eton crop, wore very disreputable clothes, and was hardly recognisable as the same person when one met her in evening dress at some function. These women knew what they were about, and did a considerable amount of cruising each season. They were of great service when the war came, at various naval stations – in charge of young W.R.N.S. girls who did ferrying duties. One of them at Warsash was known to her girls as "The Granny Wren".

The days of paid crews have gone, and nowadays the offshore racing yachts are mainly sailed by people who work in cities all the

Nichola and 'Kippy' Robinson (far left and far right) mainstays of the Hamble River Sailing Club for many years.

week and appear at weekends, or on conveniently arranged holidays, to enter the Solent Points, British Level Rating Championships, and the other club events, and perhaps the Fastnet. There is a tremendous amount of back-up work by the designers, builders, sailmakers, mast-makers and riggers, plus the firms who produce the navigational equipment.

At the bottom of the chain is the provisioning. It always stuck in my memory that Sir Alec Rose (whose 28ft lifeboat conversion *Neptune's Daughter* was at our yard before he acquired *Lively Lady* for his round the world voyage), was a firm believer in rich fruit cake as an important and nutritious part of his seagoing diet. The crew I looked after for some time didn't seem to go for that, one member had a craving for almond slices, which regularly appeared on my shopping list. With everyone much more conscious of food values nowadays, (long gone are the days of ship's biscuit and salt beef), the crew eat brown rolls and Granary bread, muesli, honey, nuts, raisins, a good deal of fruit, and a ration of chocolate and Mars bars. They take cartons of milk and yoghurt, and they can make hot drinks and heat soup. These racing yachts have an open interior, so there is not a separate galley, but a small stove is used to fry bacon and eggs, sausage and tomatoes, and tinned steak and tinned vegetables can be put into one large pot for stew. Bowls, plates and mugs are of the unbreakable kind, and plastic bags are vital for keeping things dry when all the boat is awash.

After a rough weekend the scene is somewhat chaotic, but by the following Friday repairs to sails and gear have been done by the experts, the First Aid box has been checked, and off they go again, eager for their tussle with the wind and the water and the other boats of their class.

WARTIME

When war was declared on that Sunday morning in 1939 we heard the announcement over the radio in Francis's car, and he said gravely to my father "Well, that is the end of the yard". But of course it was not. It was nearly the end of the season, so the yachts were brought in and laid up. There was then a very slack period during which he kept the men employed by all kinds of unprofitable enterprises, one of which was making ploughshares. These broke constantly — probably being made of the wrong kind of steel — and were brought back by the farmers to be mended.

In due course the yard was put on the Admiralty list and we received a steady stream of Landing Craft for repairs, due to mishaps during exercises, and a succession of Steam Pinnaces from Portsmouth Dockyard for overhauls. A Commando troop arrived in the village, and the bedroom over the kitchen at "Upcott" became the billet for two of these, Roger and Frank — this conveniently having a separate stair so that they could come and go on night excursions without disturbing anyone.

The troop took part in mock battles after dark with (or rather against) the local Home Guard, which was commanded by Roderick Skiff the popular landlord of the "Swan". Any bumps or bruises which manifested next day, on either side, could be attributed to their encounters the night before. The local osteopath Mr Madsen was a very active member of the Home Guard, and, I gather, egged them on to some hair-raising swims across the river in the dark as part of the exercises.

Meanwhile, in the village, the Royal Artillery moved into the largest houses, searchlights and gunsites sprang up, the Royal Marines camp appeared in the woods up-river, and Mrs Lilian Manley, the schoolmaster's wife, collected together a band of W.V.S. helpers and opened a canteen in a room partly underground at the Church Hall. This functioned every evening, and kept going throughout the war.

It was approached from above by a steep wooden staircase and we were always afraid that some of our customers with large Army boots would miss their footing in the blackout and come hurtling down onto the stone floor—but they never did . . .

Everything was very cheap—a penny (old money) for a cup of tea, and for sandwiches which we made with cheese, tinned salmon, tomatoes, cucumber, lettuce, watercress, and anything we could lay our hands on. Our customers always seemed to be hungry, in spite of the quantities of food which we imagined they had, in contrast to our meagre civilian rations. They were always madly keen on tea from a teapot, instead of urns in their cookhouses.

My mother often came to help, bringing with her a carving knife which she had used at home for years. It had a wicked blade, so supple that it would bend almost double. She usually parked this behind a pile of loaves and refused to let anyone touch it, but on one occasion, when there was a queue, an apparently responsible sailor offered to help. She warned him about the knife, but he cut himself, and we were too busy to go to his aid. Another of his mates bandaged him up, and then cut the end of the tie-up with the knife—and he was bleeding too.

They staggered off together towards the "Gents", and did not come back for a long time. We wondered if we ought to go and see if they had both collapsed, but we were frantically busy making more pots of tea and cutting sandwiches—and eventually two pale sailors came through the door.

Another regular helper at the canteen, and a neighbour of Mrs Manley, was Mrs Sarah Randall, an energetic lady who died in 1987 aged one hundred and four.

Voluntary workers can be a problem—you have to rely on their enthusiasm and willpower to keep going, and when something lasts for four years it does become quite an effort. There was of course very little else to do in the evenings, since for some time there was a raid every night, and the neighbouring towns were not very attractive in the blackout.

Margaret — the young W.V.S. helper, this chubby young fellow is now Keith Hamilton of the Southampton Evening Echo.

The most hard-working and reliable member of my particular bunch was a fifteen year old, Margaret, who lived on an isolated farm up-river, walking quite a distance across fields, and always turning up on time. She looked quite eighteen, and when there was a slight flap with headquarters about badges or something—well on into the war period anyway—and it was said that Margaret was not old enough to "belong" to the W.V.S. it seemed rather absurd after she had been helping us for so long, so we carried on regardless.

Looking back, at those months when all the preparations for the invasion were being made, and our rivers and creeks were full of landing craft, I think it is quite amazing that no-one who lived in our prohibition coastal area whispered a word about what was afoot. It just was not discussed. We all knew what a serious venture it was, and that it involved the lives of all the servicemen in boats and planes, and in the tanks which began to converge on our roads and lurk in the cover of hedgerows ready for embarkation. I remember vividly one of my dearest cousins appearing out of the blue one evening – John who had fished with me from the end of the Boom Defence Pier on the Hamble when we were children – and who now was crew of a tank "down the road". It was a brief call, Francis produced a flask of brandy (a very rare commodity) and pressed it into his hands as he went off down the hill, leaving us wondering what fate had in store for him.

Gradually we raised enough money to buy a radio, sundry games, and an old piano, and when a good pianist appeared for a few weeks he was much in demand. Dances were held twice a week in the hall above, but many of the men still sat in the canteen, talking, reading, and producing worn snapshots of their wives, children, and sweethearts, and looking at the photographs of the helpers' sons and husbands who were far away. It became very much a place for mutual confidences and companionship in those dark days. Often we dived into ditches on the way home, when enemy planes were overhead, but we were always carefully escorted, and the blackout was full of friendly voices. As it was rated to be a country area we had no shelters, but the enemy bombers regularly passed over on their way, guided on moonlit nights by the reflection in the rivers Hamble, Itchen, and Test, which made Southampton an easy target. We did not welcome moonlight. One of the boatsheds at the yard was lost, with the vessel in it, and one night the fir trees in "Greywell" garden, next to our cottage, were ablaze with incendiaries. My cousin Betty who was then a young nurse at the Royal South Hants Hospital in Southampton was with us, and she and I sat on the floor and clutched one another. . . . Father drove her back to the hospital next morning through streets littered with glass and debris. She said it was much less frightening in the hospital underground, than in our unprotected situation.

Eventually – it seemed a very long time – we could see from our rooftop the Landing Craft gathered in the Solent – and then they were gone, and the heavy troop-carrying planes droned over on their way to France. But the great thrill was to see the first planes coming back with lights on, after all those nights of darkness. We threw open the windows and removed the shutters – and in flew thousands of beetles. Presumably they had hatched just in time for victory, and had never seen illuminations before.

It is interesting now to reflect on how healthy everyone seemed to be during the war, on the meagre rations of a few ounces per week of the basic things, sugar, butter, cheese, meat. Tinned food was on a points system. Bread, milk, soap, and clothing were rationed. Anyone getting married went around begging coupons from ancient relatives who might be expected to "make do" themselves with clothes from their pre-war past.

Young children had never seen a banana, and sweets were rationed. I was very intrigued that a large box of "Black Magic" chocolates came by post each Christmas, which was a considerable sacrifice on the part of the sender, whoever it was. Frank Paton-Moore was as curious as I was, and we examined the string and paper, the always illegible postmark, and the printing, under the office magnifier, all to no avail. It was some time after the war that someone said to me "It's Black Magic", and laughed, and then I knew.

Probably everyone was so relieved to be alive each morning that they had no time to dwell on imaginary ailments – and they ate powdered-egg omelettes, and cake made of grated carrot, and all the vegetables and fruit which could be grown and gathered.

The only crockery available in the shops was plain white "Utility", and when Harrods and various other stores stocked a dinner service after the war, with delightful Hugh Casson drawings of little Riviera scenes of harbours and boats, I bought one because it was so charming. I was amused some time later to hear one of our clients, who was getting rather short-sighted – lamenting that his wife had bought "some new plates" and he said, "I keep chasing a piece of meat which turns out to be part of the pattern''. I knew exactly what he meant – the drawings were different, but in all of them there was one fishing boat with a brown hull exactly the colour of a well done piece of beef. . . .

Mother interrupted in a little weeding.

I wrote a good many articles for gardening periodicals about that time, on the lighter side of this occupation – for instance in *Gardener's Chronicle* when Roy Hay illustrated the script with Orchard's comical drawings.

Mother and I sometimes planted something on top of what the other had put in, but mainly we managed quite amicably, and when she died at eighty-two I found how much her little daily wandering around, picking off dead flowers and pulling up a weed when she saw it, had helped to keep the garden trim. The grass always needed cutting, weeds flourished, and I fought the jungle single-handed for quite a time. There was also cooking, and my full time job at the boatyard. However, dear Mrs Hodder appeared, taking pity on me, and came to help in the house until she died suddenly, leaving her family and friends quite stunned and utterly bereft.

When we first moved to the cottage it had mains water and a very efficient drainage system from the old estate, but no gas or electricity. This did not worry mother, who had some large paraffin lamps and a Rippingille yacht cooker. So for many years she continued in the same fashion, ignoring such things as vacuum cleaners, electric irons, heaters, fires, or blankets. We had open fires, and were blissfully unaware of power cuts. Radio and large lantern torches were battery operated. Her original excuse was that she did not want her garden disturbed, but when it was pointed out that electricity could come on overhead cables she avoided the issue. She would not venture to touch any gas cooker with its array of taps, and when Hester, our nearest neighbour, left the cats' fish on the electric stove and smoke began to drift out of the windows, mother went in and removed the saucepan, but the plate continued to glow until its owner returned from her sail.

The visitor who most delighted in these simple old-fashioned ways of going on, was one of her brothers-in-law, whose own home had all the best of modern methods, and whose standard of cooking was very high. He would make a beeline for our kitchen, dragging in his wake any newcomer who had not seen it, and would stand in admiration before the Rippingille – which certainly cooked everything splendidly. "Look at that", he would say, and beam at my mother, complimenting her most sincerely after the meal which followed.

Our main problem was shades for the lamps when any of these

were broken. In wartime and post-war days there was very little to buy, and I did the rounds of junk shops in the neighbouring towns, and tried ironmongers and hardware stores, preferably in country districts where there still might be some anciet stock. I wrote to Davey & Co, the Yacht Chandlers in the East India Dock Road, whose old catalogue showed such items as "Opal Globes for Saloon Lamps", but they replied regretfully that these were no longer imported. We had one piece of good fortune—a friend ran to earth (literally) two glass shades, one pink and one white, which had been used in a garden as cloches. With the soil washed off they were as good as new, and recieved with great pleasure by my mother. I also found a white globe on top of a dustbin outside a house which was being cleared of furniture. In those days we had no shame.

As a footnote to the paraffin cooking, these stoves need air—which in a yacht they would get from a skylight in the galley. Our kitchen too had a skylight, and this took out the fumes. In fact the cottage had several skylights, all of which leaked at certain times, depending on the direction of the wind and rain—and no builder ever seemed able to cure the leaks permanently. There were hazards during the hours of darkness as we wandered about bearing aloft lighted lamps and keeping a good look out for basins on the floors of the passages to catch drips. Years later I had the skylights taken out and the spaces roofed in, but we lived with them for a very long time.

In the early nineteen fifties some of the men I knew were writing articles for the yachting press and it occurred to me that I might well do the same, so I sent a contribution on *Life in a Boatyard* to the "Trident & Blue Peter" which was a shipping periodical published monthly in Leadenhall Street. This was accepted, and they continued to take illustrated articles from me. I also wrote a yachting column for a glossy—*Savoire Faire*. This and *Hampshire* magazine used very good paper, which is satisfactory because it maintains the quality of the photographs. If you go to a lot of trouble to take good clear black and white pictures, and they are reproduced on newsprint quality paper, the result is very diappointing.

Fishing boats have a particular appeal. One late evening at Oban the fleet came in, with clouds and a sunset behind them, and these are some of my most treasured photographs. A cousin who was with me, complaining bitterly of the cold (which I unkindly ignored), took some comfort afterwards because, although it was July, one of the shots was printed later with a caption by the Editor—"A Winter Scene on the Quay". . . . Subsequently a Scottish firm of rope and rigging makers used it as their calendar. Another satisfactory "catch" was when some French fishing boats were sheltering from bad weather at Ramsgate, and the crews were allowed ashore via Jacob's Ladder,

Some photographs I have used in this and other books were taken by Leslie Smith, who first came to us at Deacon's Yard in 1940 in his capacity as Admiralty Engineering Inspector. All the firms who were engaged on naval contracts from Portsmouth Dockyard were visited regularly—for consultation on the action to be taken after engines had been stripped down, or hulls surveyed, for subsequent progress of jobs, and eventually for trials in Southampton Water with the respective dockyard representatives aboard.

After the war he was appointed to a new engineering depot at Fareham, and then continued his absorbing hobby—photography. Film was still very difficult to obtain, and we used many peculiar makes, with varying results, until supplies were back to normal—in black and white—colour came later. Cameras were not automatic or "instamatic" as now, and the speed and aperture, etc., had to be worked out according to the conditions prevailing. It was also a constant battle to find a processor who produced good contrasty prints and enlargements—"wishy-washy" ones went flying back with notes of protest. He was extremely critical of poor work, in any field.

When I wrote *Hampshire Coast Ways* Adlard Coles asked for

'A Winter Scene on the Quay'. July, 1953.

assistant appeared in my office doorway at the yard and I knew that something was wrong. He had been found that morning, having died in his sleep.

The publicity from *Hampshire Coast Ways* had spin-offs, such as inclusion in a B.B.C. book programme on radio, and invitations to speak at meetings, one of which was from the Southampton Master Mariners Club, which in those days met for a monthly luncheon in the ballroom at the end of the Royal Pier. Proffering the money for the car pier toll, the attendant returned sixpence to me, remarking "Master Mariners and Wooden Legs half price". . . . Did some kindly councillor once decree that retired seafarers should be allowed this concession, enabling them to sit on the pier and watch the ships? Nowadays the Mariners gather in a building in St. Michael's Square, so they are not far from the water.

The shore end of the pier, which resembles in style the Prince Regent's Pavilion at Brighton, has now become a restaurant. The seaward end with the ballroom caught fire in 1987 and was destroyed.

Across the road is the handsome white building which once housed the Royal Southern Yacht Club — before their move to Hamble. In 1987 it was used for a cocktail party celebrating the Club's foundation, one hundred and fifty years ago.

Nearby is the Pilgrim's memorial — the fathers set off from here before finally departing from Plymouth, and there is also a memorial to Mary Ann Rogers, brave stewardess of the *Stella*, a cross channel ship wrecked on the casquets while on passage from Southampton to Guernsey.

Some five years after the war had ended we noticed Americans amongst our prospective buyers of boats, and we found from conversation with them that they had been "all over" looking for bargains. This trend continued throughout the fifties, and one of the interesting cases which came to our notice was when one Ed Scheller found a boat named *Solace II* in the yard of our neighbours

about seventy photographs, so we sent him our combined efforts, and by chance those chosen worked out at exactly the same number from each camera, so honours were even. Leslie did some very good work which was used for magazine covers, but that book was the only one in which he knew of his inclusion because one day his

Primmer & Snook, took it back to the States, and subsequently sold it to Bob Sweinhart of Redondo Beach, California.

We all helped Mr Sweinhart with his enquiries to trace the history of the yacht, and the following emerged:-

A Mr H.E. Peel of Catisfield House near Fareham in Hampshire owned an 1865 Brixham Trawler or smack, 38ft long and rigged as a gaff top'sl yawl. She was named *Solace*. Mr Peel commissioned a Mr H.P. Blake, M.I.N.A. who was located at 70, High Street, Southampton, to scale up the lines of *Solace* to a more modern design. This gave 48ft on deck, plus a 10ft bow-sprit, and in 1901 William Watty of Fowey in Cornwall was given the order to build *Solace II*, which the American owner wrote "is and will remain a floating tribute to English design and craftsmanship". He continued "The materials, time for craftsmanship, motivation for perfection, and real pride, are in my opinion no longer available to duplicate *Solace II* from available natural materials and today's standards of workmanship". He went on to say "All that lives is not just humans; there are also animals, plants, fishes, and what we have created by our best efforts. And these efforts deserve recognition, preservation, and

Southampton. Memorial to Mary Ann Rogers, brave stewardess of the "Stella", and on right the Pilgrim Fathers' Memorial.

Southampton. The old Harbour Board building at Town Quay.

Mr. & Mrs. William Watty of Fowey. He built "Solace II". The photograph marked their Diamond Wedding in 1933.

Courtesy James Turpin

remembrance".

What praise for this boatbuilder from Fowey and those who worked for him.

Mr Watty died in 1949, but James Turpin who worked with him and was for some time Coxswain of the Fowey Lifeboat, very kindly allowed me to have a copy of the photograph taken when William Watty and his wife celebrated their diamond wedding. Their son, A.H. Watty continued with the yard until his death, after which James Turpin ran it until he was obliged to give it up in 1983 because of osteo-arthritis. One of the last boats built—in 1981—was

a 41ft schooner to a Murray Peterson design, which he says should—like *Solace II*—carry on for generations.

The various owners of *Solace II* were traced, and in the meantime Mr Sweinhart proceeded with improvements and reconditioning— apparently to the exclusion of all his other commitments, for writing in 1979 he said "As we start our summer season *Solace* has a new Perkins diesel, new teak deckhouse, two new 2-speed winches, and a new cockpit—and I start with a new pair of swimming trunks—I can no longer afford clothes. . . ."

However, things improved. In 1985 he wrote "After five years of winter restoration and summer playing with *Solace*, she rewarded me with sheer enjoyment by her performance and reliability. She won, or was placed, in every classic design race entered, consistently beating boats half her weight and age".

A very satisfied owner one might say.

The Chandlery at Deacons entrance, alongside the A27 road, was built after Mrs Sheridan took over the old Primmer & Snook Yard. It was opened, as "Neptune's Locker" by Sir David Price our local M.P. At that time John Kitson was one of the directors, and lived at No.7 Greyladyes, part of the big house. John had a long association with the Hamble River, having worked for Woodnutts in Warsash for several years, and being friendly with the Fuger family who lived and fished there. He also knew the Lukes of Hamble and remembered several of the launchings at their yard. In 1968 he went to Malta to start up and manage Camper & Nicholson's business there, and stayed until Mr Mintoff refused to renew his work permit. Camper & Nicholson then appointed him as their agent for the Cote d'Azur, and he and his wife lived at Grasse. Since his retirement and the death of Mrs Kitson he has lived in Nice, and has worked as an independent surveyor and yacht consultant. He sounds very settled there.

Meakes of Marlow later took over the Bursledon chandlery as their South Coast branch, and continued until 1985 when the

Sir David Price, M.P. opening the new Chandlery 'Neptune's Locker' at Deacons Yard in 1964.

Courtesy Sir Peter Johnson

Foulkes brothers of Riverside Yard transferred their "Aladdin's Cave" to this more prominent position.

Our old friends would find a few changes in the bridge area now. "The Swan" has become a Berni Inn, the "Red Lion" at Swanwick has become the "Spinnaker", and when lit up at night looks like a roundabout—(a carousel), from the other side of the river. The old cottages in Church Lane have been replaced by the Swan Flats, and what is more—the Cabin Cafe where over the years the Kendall sisters, Mrs. Slee, Mrs. Clarke, Miss Hann, Miss Cooper, and other kind ladies, supplied tea and home cooked meals to wet and cold and hungry boat people has given place to a large building which is a Chinese restaurant, the Dragon Boat.

Boat owners and yard workers used to trot across the road to the Cabin Cafe, and it was not such a hazardous crossing then, with far less traffic. Reg Calvert was a regular there, and would keep me up to date with the latest gossip . . . There was a good deal of fun, and one lady who had come rather late to sailing, bored everyone with her tales of adventure, was always referred to as "Force Eight".

There were always dogs. Father had a Springer Spaniel "Sandy" who came from Sir John Thornycroft's Sandown Kennels. Francis had two black Labradors, and Mrs Deacon had "Button", a white West Highland. He was a larger dog than the present West Highlands, with a coat which stood up like wire. He loved to go ratting in the railway bank, and was often dragged out backwards by Mr Paton-Moore who was devoted to him. Then came a succession of little black chows, little cuddly bears, and in the end we had ten or more of the Cavalier King Charles's which Mrs Sheridan bred.

A dog I loved was Ella and Frank Verrill's Kim, a black and white Cocker Spaniel, who in his day enjoyed boats and had many adventures. On one occasion they went ashore for a meal at Lymington, leaving Kim safely (as they thought) on board. How he managed to wriggle himself out they never knew, but when they returned there was no dog. Kim had swum ashore and was lost. They trailed about the town, and at length returned miserably to a sleepless night. In the morning early they went looking again, and eventually he was found, damp and bedraggled, in a greenhouse where the finder had put him for safety for the night. In his latter days he became blind, but continued to get around with evident pleasure—he came to know my house and garden as well as his own, since he stayed with me when his owners had to go abroad. He was passionately fond of cucumber . . . and Ella said that when a neighbour of theirs had an open greenhouse, Kim had struggled through the hedge and eaten as much as he could reach of the hanging crop. My Cavalier Gypsy Moth went in for grapes, but as befitted a dog with Royal antecedents, she expected you to peel and de-seed them first, while she sat up straight and waited to be served. Mrs Deacon also had Pippa, a Kerry Blue. This descendant of a fighting breed did not do much for the reputation of her kind. She often sat in the back of my office chair, leaving me the front edge, and when strangers entered she would growl menacingly with her head over my shoulder. So much for protection . . . but what pleasure all these have brought over the years.

We always had several doctors amongst our boat-owners—it was a sure way for them to get away from telephones in those days, and one in particular was young and good-looking and a great favourite with the patients at the local Children's Hospital. This annexe of the Southampton Hospital was at a house, Brixedon, at the top of Blundells Lane which was the old road to Winchester before the present roads came into being. From Brixedon there is a view right across the Solent, and when Dr Bower took a job abroad, he arranged that a ship by which he left Southampton should sound its siren when it was in mid-Solent and in sight of the children he had looked after.

In his later years we had the artist T.C.C. Bryan at the yard, on the little yacht *Sioux*. The seascapes he painted had the most realistic breaking waves that I have seen—he was very gifted. One of the portraits he did was of an Army Commander whose chest was lavishly decorated with miniature ribbons, and he remarked afterwards that he found such tiny detail very trying, at his age. I can imagine this, since he was very meticulous and would never be satisfied with anything short of perfection.

Lands End House has had some interesting owners. Following the death of Eric Humphery, and that of his father soon afterwards, the house was purchased by James Taylor and his son, boatbuilders from the Thames. They were suceeded by Mr Costain of the world famous civil engineering firm, and subsequently by Mr Bernard J. Ellis, who had owned the *Isabel*, a converted trading ketch, built at Milford Haven in 1897, which had been moored off Lands End at Bursledon for some time. Mr Ellis had a very varied career, one time Vice-Commodore of the Royal Cruising Club, author of the Ellis Tide Charts, a pioneer oil engineer, and co-inventor of P.L.U.T.O. (Pipe Line Under The Ocean) in the war. He also shone in another direction, inviting his neighbours to an occasional buffet supper, at which he served most succulent cold chicken. On enquiry, he explained to me that the trick was to put raw apple inside the birds, so that they did not get dry in the cooking. . . .

COWES

The Isle of Wight has always been a familiar place to me because from the time when I was a baby we made a monthly journey from our waterside village to Southampton, and thence by the old paddle steamers to Cowes. *Princess Helena, Princess Beatrice*, the *Prince of Wales*, and *Her Majesty*—Queen Victoria and all the Royal family gave their names to the boats which ambled down Southampton Water and across the Solent. My father held me up to show me the "gingerbeer" churned up by the paddles, and we went to look at the huge polished cranks of the engines rising and falling and smelling of hot oil, and to see the crew's dinner of meat, potatoes, and cabbage, cooking over a bright coal stove in the little galley. In the passengers' dining saloon the white tablecloths and napkins were stiff with starch, and the green water splashed against the ports. Many of the old paddlers ran for seventy years or so before they were finally taken off service. Sometimes it was very rough, and sometimes the passage was smooth—my mother disliked it any way. If she and I were left behind to stay with the grandparents, and had to return on our own, she was always vastly relieved if we found a certain lady on board. The lady was large and motherly, and one of the shareholders of the old Southampton and Isle of Wight Steam Packet Company. She wore a sailor hat of black straw, and my mother sat beside her and was reassured. When there was something interesting to see, the passengers on the ferries would crowd to the rail, and this alarmed my mother, who would go to the other side of the ship in the touching belief that her seven stones would correct the list. . . . On this question of "trim", one of her rather plump young sisters was flattered when asked by two lads to go with them in a race at one of the regattas. She murmured that she didn't know much about sailing, to which they replied brightly "Oh, that doesn't matter, what we really need is ballast".

Marks became familiar—Netley Castle, Netley Hospital, Calshot Castle, the Lightship, Black Jack. I loved the twinkling lights of the buoys at night. Sometimes the paddler eased up at Calshot, and service men were put aboard from a launch. Later, when my father was in the Royal Naval Air Service he sometimes joined us in this way.

Southampton Water was clean in those days. The forest shore was green and unspoilt—no Fawley Refinery, no Power Station, no installations of any kind.

On landing at Cowes we often called in to see my father's uncles, Edward and William Ritchie, who had an office upstairs from the Pontoon, approached by a doorway under the archway as you go out into Cowes High Street. The window was a very good vantage point. In those days you might look down and see Queen Mary going by slowly in a Rolls-Royce, or Princess Mary and one of the princes dashing along towards the Royal Yacht Squadron and trying to escape notice. In Cowes Week you might see almost anyone of the most notable people of Europe at that period.

Great Uncle Edward was Overseer for Cowes—that is he was responsible for collecting the rates, and he was assisted by his brother William. They lived at Gurnard, with my eldest aunt, Elizabeth, as their Housekeeper. Uncle Edward's wife, Julia Laslett, had died, and Uncle William was a bachelor. My grandparents lived nearby. The three brothers were always quick to see the funny side of things, and they told me, as a little joke, that the trains at

Great-uncle Edward Ritchie who was Overseer at West Cowes, assisted by his brother William.

Cowes were kept upstairs—as indeed they were when you approached the railway station from the sea level High Street. The High Street was often flooded on spring tides, and still is. Of their contemporaries a few names remain—Benzie the Jeweller, Pascall Atkey, Ships Chandlers, Damant & Son, Solicitors, Beken the world famous photographers of yachts, Ratsey the Sailmakers, Lallow, Yacht Builders.

Most of the Isle of Wight Railway has been closed, but in its heyday it was the subject of the usual jokes about passengers being able to get out and pick flowers on the way. It was however a very personal service, and I have heard my great-uncles say that Mr Albert Edward Marvin, who at that time was one of the important business men in Cowes, travelled daily between his house at Carisbrook and his office. The train would be waiting in the station (upstairs . . .) for the homeward run, and matters would be timed so exactly that

A.E. Marvin would march along the platform, enter his compartment, the flag would be waved, the whistle blown, and the train would start. It was unthinkable that he should ever be delayed or that it should leave without him.

There were still a few horse-cabs on the rank, and we would either jog out to Gurnard in one of these, or have a ride in one of the new taxis. I liked to walk round the shore, but the grownups were not very enthusiastic; the Esplanade did not go very far, and the greater part of the way you were on the beach, avoiding rocks and occasional patches of "Blue Slipper". Then you had to climb up from the shore to Worsley Road.

Father (Robert Ritchie), Mother, and myself and our dog Sandy at Gurnard in 1911.

Ann Ritchie, at Gurnard in about 1895.

Gurnard was a very quiet place in those days—no beach huts and no hotels on the shore. I well remember the outcry about the beach huts, "spoiling the place". The cliffs to the west, beyond the marsh, had countless wild flowers, those exquisite miniatures which grow under such windswept conditions.

My Scottish great-grandfather had come to the Island from France—I never knew what he was doing there, but France had many links with Scotland in the old days. His parents must have lived in London when he was young, because he and his sister Caroline Lavinia, were christened at St. Clement's Dane in the Strand. At first he had Gurnard Farm, and then bought land and built a house in Worsley Road. At some stage in these events a North Sea pilot named William Cubitt came to Cowes to live in retirement, bringing with him his niece Ann. Ann is reported to have said that there were only men in the sailing ship by which they came, and it was very rough. She brought with her a large hand-woven tablecloth with the Kentish "Invicta" crest, (still in use). William Cubitt soon lost his housekeeper—to my great-grandfather, and they had three sons, of whom my grandfather Robert was the eldest. When I remember him he was quite old, and spent much of his time reading. He was a great admirer of Charles Dickens, and heartily approved of the good work of exposing the cruelty and mismanagement of many of the institutions of that period. One oddity—he could not not bear anthems. He said you went to church to worship, not to be entertained—and whenever there was an anthem he got up and walked out, to signify his disapproval. . . . The other scene in which I remember him was on a stepladder in the greenhouse, spectacles on nose, and in his hand a pair of those long thin grape scissors which thinned out the bunches. It was a large Black Hamburg vine, and most time-consuming if you were to harvest bunches of large grapes. There were hanging baskets of maidenhair fern which needed constant watering, and there was a lovely damp earthy scent.

Great Uncle Edward was a churchwarden, organised choir outings, and was a very hospitable man. When he came to Southampton he bought me Turkish Delight, and, at Easter, chocolate eggs from Richard Allen's shop at Bargate. I was very puzzled to find fluffy yellow chicks inside the eggs, and could not imagine how it was done. Great Uncle William was very quiet, and his hobby was growing prize carnations, so he was quite happy to stay at home. They all got on very well together, and addressed one another with old-fashioned courtesy, as Robert, Edward, William, and my grandmother Susannah. They were all convinced of the special excellence of the air at Gurnard, but they did make visits to cousins in Kent sometimes in the summer. Grandfather told me that he went on one of the first trains from Southampton to London, with open carriages.

The great-uncles knew all the local characters, and one of their stories was of twin brothers who bought a small-holding and went to a cattle dealer, rather an artful customer, on a Sunday, and asked if he could sell them a few pigs. The dealer looked at them in pretended horror, and in righteous accents said "Not on the Sabbath, my sons. Come back on Monday and I'll talk to you". "For", said he, afterwards, "I didn't have a pig in the place you see, but I got out the old trap and by Monday morning there they were". . . .

Islands are fine for people with no commitments elsewhere, but fog and severe gales can play havoc with travel. All these old people died in winter months, so that my father had some journeys in appalling weather. One of my aunts married a Clan Line skipper, and when he was due to rejoin his ship at Liverpool or elsewhere he would come to us on the mainland the day before, so that he would be able to set off by train, without hazard of fog stopping the steamer service. The service was also suspended during the coal strike—as the paddlers had coal-fired steam engines. We were on the Island trying to get home, but father discovered one of the Gosport launches at Cowes, and we came across to Southampton

Grandfather Robert Ritchie about 1870.

never was put to the test.

Coming into Cowes on the ferry the church which can be seen is Holy Trinity, but the Parish church is St. Mary's. From the Esplanade you need to walk up Castle Hill behind the Royal Yacht Squadron, and then through an archway and up a flight of steps into Northwood Park. St. Mary's is in the trees, beside Northwood House. The original was built in 1657 as West Cowes Chapel, but it was not consecrated until after restoration of the Monarchy in 1662. It was rebuilt, except the tower, in 1867, and is quite large, seating nearly a thousand people. Charles Wesley preached there in 1735, and Dr Arnold, Headmaster of Rugby, was baptised there in 1795. Northwood House was presented to the town in 1929 by Mr & Mrs Wilfrid Ward, and is now used as offices by the Medina Borough Council.

on that. The man in charge appealed for help as he did not know Southampton, so father piloted him in to the Town Quay where we disembarked.

After his retirement Great-Uncle William kept his watch and clocks at the "proper" time, and never altered them forward or back, and it did not inconvenience him at all. In fact the only complaint which any of the family had with the Island life was that everything was more expensive there. And of course prisoners did occasionally escape from Parkhurst. One old lady, Miss Minnie Price, kept a bowler hat on a peg in her hall, so that any intruder would be frightened? by the thought of a man in the house. . . . As a deterrent to a possibly desperate escapee this does seem rather an impossibly optimistic idea. . . . Fortunately for Miss Minnie it

Grandmother Susannah Ritchie about 1870.

Cowes. "St. Mary's" the Parish Church, in Northwood Park.

Cowes. Northwood House, – now offices of the Medina Borough Council.

There are some splendid old cedars and other trees in the park, and the whole area is very well maintained, which perhaps would not have been the case had it been in private owership now.

One of Great Uncle Edward's churchwardenly stories was of a vicar who returned after a long absence, and said in his address how nice it was to see "so many old Cowes faces", which was perhaps not the most tactful way of putting it. I don't know whether this was at St. Mary's or at Holy Trinity. . . .

It was a pity the great-uncles were no longer alive to see the antics of the Cowes character, Uffa Fox, as I am sure they would have been vastly amused by his successful efforts to evade tax on his converted floating bridge, which he bought in 1925 and used as a home and office in the days of his first marriage. As the River Medina flows through four parishes—East Cowes, West Cowes, Whippingham, and Northwood, near its mouth, Uffa had the floating bridge towed around until the tax people were defeated in their efforts to bring him to book. It was a great lark.

The pink boathouse on the waterfront was his abode in later years, when he was honoured with the presence of Prince Philip, Prince Charles, and many famous people.

The inscription on the pillar by the steps at the Royal Yacht Squadron—at the other end of the town—indicates that the landing place is for use of members of the R.Y.S. and persons engaged on H.M. service only, and with so many Royal personages present in Cowes Week in days gone by there was very strict adherence to all the rules. Anyone engaged in "trade" had very little chance of becoming a member of that exclusive club.

The years during which Queen Victoria lived at Osborne undoubtedly helped the business people, who vied for patronage, and I see that an 1860 photograph of my grandmother—by Brown & Wheeler of Cowes—announces on the reverse side that they are under the immediate patronage of Her Most Gracious Majesty the Queen, and the court at Osborne.

People of my generation may remember the toyshop near the Esplanade at Cowes—belonging to Miss Minnie and Miss Flo

Clarke. Miss Minnie always went to London on a buying expedition just before Christmas, and came back with beautiful dolls and all kinds of exciting toys. One year she had a fall and broke her thigh, and was in a London Hospital for the weeks which such an injury entailed in those days. The two ladies were old friends of my aunts, so we never passed the shop without going in, and for some reason which I cannot explain I was quite terrified. My dearest wish was to have a "proper" dolls pram (which I never did), and in spite of being allowed to push one of these elegant carriages up and down the shop I cried inconsolably all the time—to the great embarrassment of my mother. The only reason I can think of now is that old Mrs Clarke was deaf, and Miss Flo had to shout to make her hear, and people with loud voices always frightened me.

Cowes. The Royal Yacht Squadron Landing, with the Royal Yacht lying off. (1953).

Another member of the Gurnard group of expatriate Scots was a Miss Beata Macaulay. It seems that she came to stay with my great-grandparents for the good health (that Island air . . .) and remained for the rest of her life. She was godmother to my aunt Elizabeth, and a letter she wrote while on a visit to Winchester—referring to my father as "little Bobby", has survived.

She wrote a good deal of verse, one little book dated 1869 published by Sampson Low, Son & Marston of Crown Buildings, Fleet Street, and printed by Whittingham & Wilkins of Took's Court, Chancery Lane—contains "The Newtown Rats" and two others. This began—

"In Thirteen Hundred Seventy-Seven
A most unpleasant thing occurred,
The French, fermenting with the leven
Of pride, to mischief inly stirred,
Descended on the Isle of Wight
And anchored thick in Franchville Bay,
Captured the town, few showing fight,
Sacked, slaughtered, burnt, and sailed away".

It goes on to relate that in time the people built Newtown, but in the reign of Edward III it became so rat-ridden that they offered £100 to a wandering piper, and the rest of the story is much as the tale of the Piper of Hamelyn. I very much doubt if the latter part is true, but of course the French did destroy the original town, and there is hardly anything left but stones under the grass.

Considering all the damage the French did in the Isle of Wight long ago, it is somewhat ironic that the Free French ships which had escaped the Germans in the 1939/45 War were directed to Cowes as their base when they arrived in England. I have one of the badges which they gave to people who helped them—it was earned by one of my friends, now dead, and is a red cross of Lorraine on a blue enamel background, with the words "France Libre" on it. An interesting relic.

Miss Beata Elizabeth Macaulay, who wrote 'The Newtown Rats' in 1869.

One afternoon when the flood tide was running strongly a boat came up-river, turned in to the tide, and was made fast alongside another on one of our moorings off the yard at Bursledon. Presently a man rowed ashore, came up the steps into our houseboat office, introduced himself as Ben Chapman from Cowes, and sat down. He had come across the Solent and appeared to be in no hurry to come to any particular point or reason for his visit. He had a gentle face, blue eyes, and a curly brown beard, touched with gold as by the sun.

We never did get to the why and wherefore of his appearance on our side of the water, and eventually he took his leave—a most friendly meeting it had been. A few months later I read in the Isle of Wight County Press that he had died, aged something over seventy, but that was all we knew.

When at Cowes, I asked Mr Beken (who presides over the world famous business dealing with photographs of all the large racing yachts which ever graced the Solent, and were captured by his father with a plate camera in the early days), if he knew Ben Chapman. "Yes", he said, "he was a masthead man". Mr Beken rifled through one of their large books of photographs, and showed me exactly where the masthead man perched when those magnificent yachts were racing with all their sails spread. There would be sails all around him, above and below, and he would be quite alone, high up, with the sun and wind and whatever weather chanced that day.

Mr Beken added that Ben later kept the Standard, which is uphill from the town, opposite Northwood Park. Beken is a name which has added to the prestige of Cowes in yachting circles world wide, and it all began with A. E. Beken who opened a chemist's shop in the reign of Queen Victoria. The Queen, then living at Osborne House, gave the business royal patronage, and the foreign royalties and wealthy people who came to Cowes Week in their magnificent yachts, followed suit.

The son, Frank Beken, yearned to capture the beauty of the huge yachts of those days, and in the beginning he ventured out in a very small boat, holding a primitive plate camera. The photographs which he took are unique, and are to be seen in the vast collection held by the family, and reproduced in books and calendars.

The present photographers, Keith Beken and his son Ken, have a fast launch for the Solent, and they sometimes use a helicopter to take shots from above racing craft. They travel abroad, wherever the Tall Ships go, or when some important race makes coverage desirable. Nowadays much more of their work is for commercial purposes than by selling single copies to individual owners, because costs are high and the business must pay. They work long hours, and at the end of the day afloat the cameras have to be taken apart and cleaned of salt. The film is processed and the results scrutinised closely.

Ken has a toddler – and no doubt he will soon be taken out with them, to become accustomed to the chase, and to learn how to shadow without getting in the way of any of the competitors – a technique which his predecessors have mastered so successfully.

The waterfront of the Medina is closely packed with yards and allied concerns, there are two marinas and the International Sailing Centre. On the East Cowes side is Westland Hovercraft and the Trinity House Yard with bright coloured buoys lined up, and between the two halves of the town shuttles the Floating Bridge with an enormous International Paints advertisement on each side of it.

One of the most essential services at Cowes is the rigging dealt with by Harry Spencer's firm. And it does not stop there; he undertakes work wherever the need arises. After the *Mary Rose* was raised from beneath the Solent, Harry's men were responsible for securing her in her cradle at the Dockyard, to make sure she did not move.

In January 1987 the replica of a traditional Omani Dhow arrived at Portsmouth on the deck of a German cargo vessel, was unloaded and towed across to Cowes by Spencers, to be completely fitted out and rigged. The Dhow which is 115ft long x 28ft beam x 24ft from keel to deck was built on a beach at Mubarak, and it is quite a compliment for the Solent workpeople that it was transported so far for their attention. Harry Spencer is a modest man who doesn't talk about his accomplishments – it is difficult to get him to discuss what he has done in his lifetime – a friend of his said to me "He carries it all in his head".

Most people would agree that the Royal Yacht Squadron at Cowes is the most exclusive yacht club, even nowadays, but since 1984 another organisation has claimed distinction. It is the South West Shingles Yacht Club, membership of which is by invitation only. Qualifications are personality and humour, and a willingness to confess to an "incident" such as going aground on the Shingles which is a bank in the Solent on which owners of many craft have found themselves. I think a worse place to go aground is Hamble Spit, since everyone passing in and out of the mouth of the river observes this shameful situation. The Shingles Bank comes into the news from time to time when on particularly low tides sundry eccentric cricketers go out there and attempt to have a game before they are washed away.

During the war the yard of J.S. White on the Medina built a great number of vessels – destroyers, frigates, motor torpedo boats, and a variety of landing craft. The older people at Cowes still remember the raid of April 28th, 1942, when Messerschmitt fighter/bombers flew in low. There was a good deal of damage at Saunders-Roe (now British Hovercraft premises) and at J.S. White's, and sixty-seven civilians killed. Damage and casualties would have been greater had it not been for the Polish Destroyer *Blyskawica* which was lying off, and put up a barrage of anti-aircraft fire. The Poles were held in great esteem for their contribution to the defence of the town and it is good to know that the ship is still well maintained in their own country.

Soon after the Great War ended Sir Mansfield Cumming who had been the Commanding Officer at the Boom Defence, and later the first Captain "C" of the British Secret Service, died in London, before he could move to his new house Bursledon Lodge. The boatshed on Salterns Marsh and the machinery and equipment collected over the years was in father's charge, and in 1921 there was an auction sale to which people came from all over the country. Bentleys and Bugattis lined the narrow lanes. Amongst the strange lots was an enormous caterpillar tank, which seemed quite a useless object – it only crawled at a snail's pace – but someone bought it.

In a recent Timewatch Programme on Captain "C" there was a mention of the scooter which he had made after he lost his leg in the car crash in which his son Alistair was killed. On this scooter he rested his artificial leg and whizzed along the corridors of the London H.Q. He was a very inventive man.

The next owner of Bursledon Lodge was Mr. Noel Van Raalte from Brownsea Island. He was interested in the new type of boats — which were stepped, and planed on the surface of the water, and he did a great deal of experimental work on this, being associated in a friendly way with Hubert Scott-Paine, who by that time had established his British Power Boat Company at Hythe and was preparing for his success in 1933 when he broke the water speed record with *Miss Britain III* at just over 100 m.p.h. Father supervised the work in the marshland boatyard, arranged supplies of material and was very interested. On Saturdays we often went to Hythe Pier to watch the performance of the latest boat. Firmly fixed in my memory is that one day a box no larger than a biscuit tin was put down beside me on the planking, and from it came music. The first portable wireless I had seen. Pure magic. . . . After all these years I still consider it is magic. . . .

YARMOUTH

Yarmouth at the western inside edge of the Isle of Wight was always a favourite objective of people sailing from the Hamble River, particularly in the days when it was much less crowded.

Wing Commander A. F. Somerset-Leeke had interesting memories of it from his boyhood in his father's steam yacht. He first went there in 1893 when all cargo for Lymington was carried in flat-bottomed boats which were warped out to the pier and towed across by the paddle steamer *Mayflower*. He said he had seen carriages with the owners seated in them, complete with coachman and groom, transported thus. What a sight. . . .

The piermaster for many years, named Warder, would ring a bell for the departure of the ferry, and call out "Hurry up. Any more for

Mr. Noel van Raalte at Bursledon, about 1930.

Yarmouth, Isle of Wight.

Photo Frank Verrill

England", and, said the Commander, "that wasn't meant to be funny". The Islanders took themselves and their Island very seriously. I remember my own elderly grandparents and great-uncles and aunts, who lived at Gurnard—were convinced that the air was much better than on the mainland—and with the Isle of Wight sitting out in the English Channel and open to all the winds—it probably was.

At Yarmouth Glenshane remembered old Pittis, "who lived in an upturned boat and earned an honest shilling wheeling Miss Fanny Paris, aged a hundred, in a bathchair—Spray the ex-schoolmaster who read the lesson on Sunday and lived to almost ninety-seven, and Flint the harness-maker who was reputed to be a hundred and seven, and was several times visited by Queen Mary". (Presumably when the Queen was staying on the Royal Yacht at Cowes for the Regatta and toured the Island antique shops, which she often did when King George V. was racing in the *Britannia*.)

It seems a great pity—now that interesting old ships are being collected in Portsmouth Dockyard as a tourist attraction—that, after the death of King George, *Britannia* was taken out from Cowes quietly by Naval ships, and sunk in deep water somewhere off St.Catherines Point. Much effort and money has been spent in restoring the survivors of the beautiful "J" Class yachts, and *Britannia* would have been a fine addition. Perhaps the King left instructions that no-one else was to sail her. Fifty years on, people are much more interested in preserving such unique examples of craftsmanship. The Schooner *Westward* met the same end in 1940, when the owner Mr. T. B.Davies died, and ordered this action if his trustees could not find anyone able to maintain the yacht "in the style to which she was accustomed". At that time no-one was very likely to buy her—with an attack expected at any moment. I remember *Westward* used to sail with the "J" Class yachts in the days when my father followed the progress and took me with him.

"Glenshane" also said that in those days (1893), there was a large expanse of water running eastwood round the corner of the old Mill House, and opening out at the back of the town behind a house named "The Mount." There was a small exit from this water crossed by a bridge just east of The Mount, thus making the town of Yarmouth into an island. When raids by the French were imminent, vessels could take shelter behind the town. During the eighteen-nineties, in one hard winter, the Rector, H. F.Speed, was able to sail his ice yacht there. In other winters he took it to Hatchett's Pond near Beaulieu. For anyone who thinks that a sail board is a modern invention, this Island parson had a sail shaped like a kite, which he held in his hands, and beat to windward on his skates. .

By reason of its situation the Yarmouth Lifeboat has one of the busiest stations around our coast. Strong tides rush in and out of the entrance to the Solent hereabouts, and with so many yachts in the area the crew are constantly on the alert. If anyone is injured or seriously ill they are lifted by helicopter and carried across to Haslar Hospital on the mainland.

Yarmouth was the home port of *Wanderer III*, the little yacht designed by Laurent Giles & Partners of Lymington, and built by William King Ltd., of Burnham on Crouch for Eric Hiscock, in which he and his wife Susan twice sailed round the world. *Wanderer III* was only about 30 feet overall, with a waterline of 26 feet and 6 inches, and this modest pair of Solent venturers showed just what could be achieved without a great outlay of money. The books which resulted from their voyaging are classics in the yachting library. Husband and wife were both awarded the M.B.E. for services to ocean sailing. Eric Hiscock died in 1986.

In mid-September 1987 Hayles Boatyard at Yarmouth took delivery of a yacht by an unusual means of transport. The *Panacea* went ashore on rocks below the cliffs at Kimmeridge. The Insurers and Frank Verrill the Marine Surveyor decided that the only way to get her off was by lifting her clear, and after removing the portable heavy gear they engaged the services of a Chinook helicopter which had been used from Aberdeen, transporting men to and from the oil rigs.

The Chinook flew from Scotland to Eastleigh Airport, and the next day got into position above *Panacea* and picked her up in a sling. The *Daily Telegraph* had a splendid photograph of the Chinook, below it the yacht, and below both of them Frank Verrill's Cruiser *Pipperi II*, all making for Yarmouth. Here the yacht was deposited alongside Hayles' launch, taken ashore and slipped.

Obviously there is a weight limit to such an operation, but this has added another specialist job to the "whirleybirds" exploits, which have included lowering sections onto spires and high buildings, and in Austria I have seen one carrying girders and building materials from valley floor to a site high on the mountain side. That particular machine clattered busily all day, and reminded me of a bird carrying twigs for its nest. The skill of course is with the helicopter crew, who seem to regard each new mission as a challenge.

HYTHE & CALSHOT

In 1905 the Motor Yacht Club was first established at Hythe on Southampton Water. The Commodore was the Duke of Sutherland, the Vice- Commodore—Lord Montagu of Beaulieu (father of the present Duke), Racing Commodore—Commander Mansfield Smith Cumming, and the Treasurer—Lionel de Rothschild, Esq. The entrance fee was three guineas, and the annual subscription also three guineas. My Father, who was on the Boom Defence Ship *Argo*, supervised the fitting up of a yacht, *Enchantress*, which was used as the mother ship for those long narrow motorboats which were the racing craft of those days, and the club gave him a French carriage clock, suitably inscribed and dated 1906, in recognition of his help. For years he had a half

model of *Commander* which was the boat in which captain Cumming took part in the racing. Eventually I added it to the decorations on the walls of our barge/office at Deacon's Yard, and when the barge was broken up I gave the model to the (by then Royal) Motor Yacht Club at Poole, who still have it on show, in the clubhouse.

In retrospect one can see how this little group of enthusiastic motorboat owners led the way to the British Power Boats of Hubert Scott-Paine in the thirties—also at Hythe—from which followed his successful M.T.B's and M.G.B's of the Second World War.

Nowadays the Calshot Activities Centre is well known, and well patronised by youngsters who sail, and learn to ski, and take part in many sports.

After the Tristan da Cunha Islanders were obliged to abandon their homes Calshot received many of them, and no doubt they found it a familiarly windy and bleak situation.

In the early part of this century Hythe had no factories, no refinery, and no waterside marina village such as the one which has been constructed recently on reclaimed mudland. The pier and ferry has been in operation for a long time, and this is a great boon, saving commuters and other passengers from a long journey around the top of Southampton Water, through Totton and Millbrook. The ferry lands them at the Town Quay, which is most convenient.

On the west side of the water there is Eling Basin which has a working mill, attracting many visitors, and a beautiful old church. There is Cracknore Hard with that very long established boatyard, Husbands', and there is Ashlett Creek with the "Jolly Sailor" and the old Water Mill which is the headquarters of the Esso Sailing Club.

SOUTHAMPTON

There are guided tours around the old parts of Southampton, starting from Bargate, twice a day in the summer, and it is worth while going on one of these. Much has been discovered since the blitz, in which—fortunately, the oldest (and I think the best) church, St. Michaels, survived. It has one of the few black marble fonts from Tournai, and two very special lecterns, one of which came from Holy Rood. My early memory of Holy Rood is of the blind man who sat by the railings there, for whom my mother would give me some coins. The shell of this church now contains the Merchant Navy Memorial.

The Tudor House in St. Michael's Square is open to the public, and in recent years the garden has been laid out as it would (or should) have been when it belonged to Sir Richard Lyster, Lord Chief Justice of England. There is a knot garden, and old roses which are usually at their best in June. Also there are the remains of a Norman house. The new construction around St. Michael's Square fits in very well. It was quite amazing that the church was comparatively unscathed by the bombing when so much of the town was destroyed. I shall never forget the sight of practically every building in the main street reduced to rubble, or leaning walls with nothing inside them. But, as we have seen, this was not the first time it had happened—and now all has been restored. Bargate, and the old walls, and God's House Tower, and all the ancient stonework still stands, with new neighbours.

With the considerable interest in Jane Austen amongst Americans one should perhaps mention that she stayed at the Dolphin Hotel in High Street, no doubt while arrangements were being made for moving into the house in Castle Square, where she lived with her mother and sister for a time. The photographs of the Avenue by the Cowherds Inn illustrates how rural then were parts which now are within minutes of the City Centre.

As a small child I saw Southampton chiefly by reason of going through on our way to the pier for frequent visits to Cowes, and occasional shopping expeditions with my mother. The best dress shop then, was Mayes, just below Bargate, where a large red-haired commissionnaire held an outsize umbrella over ladies as they alighted from their motorcars. Almost next door was Richard Allen's wonderful chocolate shop, and Larbalastier where my father bought tobacoo.

My real acquaintance began in the late twenties when all the big lines, several a day, were in and out of the port.

In 1927 having taken a business training course at the Underwood School in Bernard Street (most entertainingly placed next door to the Navigation School where young officers came to study for their next ticket—and opposite a pastrycook's shop where the most delectable vanilla slices were sold . . .) the Principal sent me forth to Thomas Cook and Son's bureau at 31/32 Oxford Street, just across the road from the Terminus Station. Afterwards, when they knew me better, the men said I walked into the office looking like Minnehaha. . . I had two long braids of hair hanging in front, as I was still trying to get my parents' consent to have it cut. Incidentally, after a few weeks at this job I went through Luce's beautiful bow-windowed scent shop at Bargate, to the salon beyond, and had it done. The hairdresser said solemnly "Now are you quite sure?"—before he started.

At Thomas Cook's my immediate chief was Christopher Wren who ran the Shipping and Freight Department. He was appropriately, like a little bird, very alert and businesslike, and we got on very well. His hobby was rifle- shooting, he had been a quartermaster in the Army in the Great War, and in due course, became a Captain in the Home Guard. He taught me how to spell "success" (which was a word I had always mis-spelled with one "c"). His letters were always announcing the "successful conclusion" of various enterprises, so it was very important to him, and he hung up a card

Southampton. The Avenue, with the Cowherds Inn on left.
Courtesy H.E. Spencer

on the cabinet in front of me until I got it right. . . . We had no more trouble with "success".

The firm handled all kinds of shipments, some of the more interesting ones I can remember being gold bullion under escort, chincherinchees which were South African flowers, white ones, which travelled in bud and came out in water after arrival in England, and which at that time were quite rare here, and crayfish tails. It seemed that only the tails of the crayfish were of any commercial vlaue. We also took charge of firearms, pending production of a certificate, or kept them until the owners went abroad again.

The two other departments dealt with travel bookings, and with banking and exchange, and as we shared the same building, and the three girls shared an office, one soon became acquainted with the doings of the whole organisation. Regular travellers through the port at that time were the Earl and Countess of Athlone (he was then Governor of South Africa), and many people used the Cape boats for Madeira where they called en route to Capetown. The passengers from Madeira usually brought back a miscellany of wickerwork, such as the type of basket chair which stood on the lawn at the Royal Yacht Squadron at Cowes when I was a child. The Cape boats, carrying mail, were very regular, leaving Southampton at four o'clock every Thursday afternoon, and coming in at 6.00 a.m. each Monday morning. At that time they were using the old *Kenilworth*, *Arundel*, *Armadale*, *Edinburgh*, and *Carnarvon* Castles, with an occasional odd one from the London service.

The cross-channel boat from Le Havre also came in at 6.00 a.m. and the uniformed men (who wore caps shaped like those of the Wagon-Lit staff) were out early and late, accompanying the money exchange people, and meeting passengers whose impending arrival had been notified to the office.

The largest ships using Southampton then, were the ex-German vessels which had been taken over by the allies, and the Atlantic service was carried on by the *Majestic*, *Olympic*, *Homeric*, *Mauretania* —

(Southampton's much loved "Maurie") *Berengaria*, and the United States *Leviathan* to name a few. Southampton was never a "bad" dockland town, but the police did have some lively times when the *Leviathan* was in port, dealing with drunken sailors. However, this was nothing like today when innocent people are assaulted, mugged, robbed and stabbed. In the thirties, anyone could walk the streets at night without fear of attack.

The Australian/New Zealand service was maintained by the *Wanganui*, *Wangoni*, *Rangitane*, *Rangitiki* and others, and the Dutch East India boats called, the *Marnix V. St. Aldegonde*, the *Johan V. Oldenbarnevelt*, (which finished her days as the burned out *Lakonia*), and the *Christian Huygens*, lovely names for lovely ships. The French and German liners *Ile de France*, *Bremen*, and *Europa* usually anchored in Cowes Roads and picked up and landed passengers by tender, and the *Normandie* had the most beautiful lines and looked superb. I remember when a small aeroplane made a landing on her foredeck and was taken on to France, the pilot getting into quite a spot of bother for his escapade.

Then there was the new white gleaming *Empress of Britain*, which I remember with all her public rooms banked with flowers for a visit by the Prince of Wales (Edward VIII). This beautiful ship was lost in the war.

Back at the office in a glass enclosure sat the General Manager, John Day. He looked almost exactly like Mr. Punch. I was told that he wished to be a jockey when he was young, but had a bad fall, which put an end to his hopes. He was very lame.

The majority of the rest of the staff were well travelled and interesting, and one of the Foreign Exchange men was also a ventriloquist, which caused us much amusement, because he used the gas jet in our office to seal up packets of currency, during the course of which operation he conducted conversation from all angles. His name was Oliver and he had red hair — rather a Danny Kaye type.

Thomas Cook's tours then were by boat and train—no package air travel, and only a small percentage of people had holidays abroad compared with the numbers who go nowadays. Winters at the office were fairly peaceful, with the booking clerks dealing out winter sunshine for the better-off clients, trips up the Amazon for the really wealthy, and individual arrangements for special people, but the summer brought a rush to get passports and tickets sent off, and the staff then worked late. The steamers to France and the Channel Islands were fully booked, and often duplicated, because the only way to go was by sea. With the same interest in common— passengers and their goods, the dockland community was very integrated, and we mixed with the shipping company staffs and the customs house people, who used the South Western Hotel for dances in the winter, nineteen thirties occasions and very happy times.

There seems to be no-one left from those days, which I suppose is understandable since I was the youngest. I recall Mike O'Leary who often went across Channel with his friend Harold Portlet, and thought it very dashing to go to the Folies Bergere. (Now we can see it on T.V. with "Miss Bluebell"). . . . There was a large young man, Guy Brightwell, who disappeared when the Japanese over-ran Singapore. Percy Woodhams, the chief cashier, had an invalid wife, and would ask me to go into dress shops for her in my lunch-time, since he was diffident about going himself. There was Jack Lewis, whose parents kept the Gate Inn, and was lost when his ship went down early in the war, and there was George Wetherill—dear George—one of the nicest of men, who stayed with Thomas Cook and Son until he retired, apart from the war period when he learnt the trade of coppersmithing. He worked in the port from 1922 until 1977, ending as chief cashier in succession to Percy Woodhams. George was a founder member of the SKAL Club, subsequently its treasurer, and finally president. . . . (SKAL was the toast, and the club was for members of travel agencies, hoteliers, shipping company people etc). When he retired, the Union Castle Line gave him and his wife Dorothy a holiday voyage to Las Palmas in recognition of his long association with the port of Southampton. Peter Wetherill, senior P.E. Lecturer at Southampton Technical College, and a keen boating man, is their son.

In 1934, after seven years, I went back to the Hamble River and the boatyard, so that was the end of my dockland experience, which I had enjoyed tremendously.

The "Queen" liners came later, and the Western Shore at Woolston was a splendid vantage point for viewing their comings and goings.

I shall never forget when the *Queen Mary* came back after the war, having survived the dangers of troop carrying. The deep sirens of the "Queens" were stirring at any time, but when the *Queen Mary* came proudly up Southampton Water with her's sounding, and all the small craft hooting, and everyone cheering, it was an occasion of great emotion and tears of joy.

Netley Abbey. The Monks Fishpond in a garden behind the ruins.

Nowadays, Weston Shore is the scene of many angling competitions. There is a sailing club, and Netley Castle is a convalescent home.

The remains of Netley Abbey stand in a lovely setting, and in a garden behind is the monks old fish-pond. Presumably they found it easier to net their Friday meals than to go fishing in Southampton Water. Through the village is the entrance to the Royal Victoria Park. The hospital, built in the time of Florence Nightingale, has been demolished, but the central chapel remains, and is used for exhibitions. The police use the officers quarters and staff houses, and the grounds make a very pleasant waterside park, which is well used.

During the 1914/18 war, the hospital was at its maximum capacity and dealt with hundreds of wounded, some of whom arrived by ship at a pier which was built out into Southampton Water. As a very small girl I remember going with my mother to a canteen run by voluntary workers in the grounds, and seeing so many men in hospital blue, some on crutches and others in wheelchairs.

At home in Bursledon, one of our neighbours was an Army doctor who walked to Netley every day across the fields, and who subsequently went to France and was killed, leaving his beautiful wife and three nice children, John, Jane and George. That really was a terrible war — more especially so because the conditions in France were so appalling. The futility and horror of it haunts me even now, when I go down through France and see the signposts to towns and villages whose names I heard from my mother, who had three brothers in the army — one killed on the Somme. Her father, my other grandfather, ran the Remount Depot at Sherborne in Dorset during that war, and it must have broken his heart to see so many horses shipped off to France to such conditions.

The most recent book on the city of Southampton is an illustrated history by Adrian Rance, a very comprehensive study. (Ensign Publications £9.95). Of the older ones the most intimate are those by the late Miss Elsie Sandell. She was a recognised authority, her father was George Washington Sandell and her brothers were consular agents in the port. She knew all the interesting townspeople of her time, and heard their personal recollections of such inhabitants as Madame Maes who lived in Westgate House, which occupied a gap in the town walls near the pier. The house was pulled down in 1897 after Madame Maes' death, and the gap made good, the shore road being continued then to the pier.

It was extremely sad to see the decline of the docks as the great liners were replaced by aeroplanes. Boat trains no longer held up progress along Canute Road, and the South Western Hotel — which was formerly right in the centre of activity — became offices for the Inland Revenue, the B.B.C., the Ministry of Transport, and other organisations. Finally the cross channel ferries departed for Portsmouth. Boarding the QE II for a journey to Cherbourg in 1980 we passed through the ghostly hall of the Ocean Terminal which had seen so many passengers embark and disembark. It seemed to be full of large faded settees on which no-one sat. It was terribly depressing — and now has been pulled down.

1986 was the one hundred and fiftieth anniversary of the purchase of 216 acres of mudland adjacent to the Town Quay, which a group of far-seeing business men made for the foundation of the original Dock Company.

However, the hope for the future is the development of the Ocean Village and Canute's Pavilion in the Eastern Docks, with houses, offices and shops — and some gaily painted covered barrows which can be wheeled around and used as selling points. The Dock itself is in use, and there is a gathering of interesting old ships. Southampton Council, with the aid of grants, bought the Tug/Tender Calshot which many people will remember was used to transport passengers to and from liners which anchored in the Solent. She was built at Woolston in 1930, and has been used in recent years off the west coast of Ireland, where she was renamed the *Galway Bay*. She is now back at Southampton, to be reconditioned, and was given a great welcome.

There is also a new development planned for the Town Quay area, which will take in the old Harbour Board building with its dome. It is good to see this being refurbished. Waterside offices and apartments are proposed and a marina. The Hythe Ferry boats use the Town Quay and so do the Blue Funnel Cruises.

The Royal Southampton Yacht Club's decision to sell their premises in Northlands Road and move into a new building in the Ocean Village, overlooking the water, seems a good one. It will be much more convenient for visiting yachtsmen and much more pleasant for members. They have had a small establishment on the Beaulieu River at Gin's Farm as well, which has made a venue for cruising, at weekends.

The Southampton Boat Show which takes place in September has always been a success, and the great advantage it has over Earls Court is that so many of the yachts are afloat at pontoons. Visitors can try out some of the craft and it is much more of an open air show, although there is quite a large exhibition under cover.

This seems to be the right place to mention Guy Cole, who for twenty-two years was "Jack Stay" Yachting correspondent of the Southampton *Echo*. His reputation won him the "Writer of the Year" trophy in 1966, and an award from the Ship and Boat Builders National Federation. In spite of paralysis in both legs from polio, he sailed his own boat single-handed, and with Commander Bill King of *Galway Blazer* made a trans-Atlantic crossing. This resulted in his book *Sailing In Irons* and he wrote many other useful classics such as *Starting To Cruise*. We often saw him at the yard for the launching of new boats, and had a great admiration for the way in which he made light of his disability, and never let it deter him.

The 140 foot square rigged sailing barque *Lord Nelson* is based at Southampton, and was named by the Duke and Duchess of York shortly before their marriage. This is a remarkable ship, specially designed for handicapped people, with lifts and hoists and accommodation for wheelchairs.

Based in the Ocean dock is the Thames sailing barge *Kitty*, 82 feet long and built in 1895. She originally carried barley and malt, continued as a working barge until 1964 and then was used for chartering. Now she has become a mobile floating restaurant.

An occasional visitor to the dock is the centenarian yacht *Amazon*, built at the Arrow Yard, Southamtpon by Tankerville Chamberlayne in 1885. She is roughly 91 feet × 15 feet × 9 feet, and has had a string of owners including George Marvin of Cowes, a notable yachtsman early this century. *Amazon* was rescued from dereliction by the late Arthur Lowe of "Dad's Army", and is now the home of son Stephen Lowe who is keeping her in splendid condition. I had hoped to link this *Amazon* with the figurehead which was in an alleyway in Falmouth in the fifties—but apparently this is far too buxom a lady for Mr. Lowe's yacht. Mr. Whitehead (the expert on figureheads) tells me that she probably came from H.M.S. *Amazon*—and has now moved to the late Sir Max Aitken's collection at Cowes.

The Terminus Station building—at which the last train arrived in 1966—has been transformed into a restaurant/nightclub. It is a handsome building, of roughly the same age as the Docks and as the National Provicial Bank at Holyrood (1833). There has been a considerable improvement in the condition of property in Oxford and Bernard Streets recently, and if you look up, (which is what the late Alec Clifton-Brown told us we must do), you will notice that many of the houses have elegant balconies and interesting rooflines. I very much hope that Dockland Southampton may soon be as attractive as Old Portsmouth.

At the foot of Bugle Street, and opposite the Pier, is the Wool House built by the Monks of Beaulieu Abbey in the latter half of the 14th century, and here the fleeces were brought, ready for export.

The Figurehead Amazon – too large for Mr. Lowe's yacht.

even though he was obliged to take the maufacture to America, from whence they came back to us via lease-lend.

The Museum has many interesting pictures, relics, and models including local craft such as the Spit Wherry, which was a 27 feet double ender, and there is the actual Itchen Ferry Boat No. 222 built by G. Cozens in 1910 at a cost of £19.00 and now restored. It seems that SU.120. *Wonder* which I photographed some years ago on the hard at Itchen Ferry was built by Don Hatcher in 1860. That one certainly didn't look its age.

Nearly all the Shipping Company offices were in Canute Road, with the old Custom House and the Post Office on either side of the main Dock Gates. If you go eastwards along Canute Road, turning left as though making for the Itchen Bridge, you will find on your right the Hall of Aviation, which houses a most interesting exhibition – not to be missed. The largest aircraft on display is the four-engined Sandringham Flying Boat, which dwarfs everything else, and over which visitors are given a guided tour. This particular machine was used in the Caribbean after the war, and was brought back when its inter-island use came to an end. The guide on the occasion when I visited was a former Flight Engineer, who went into great detail. Having seen these Flying Boats taking off down Southampton Water on many occasions when they were based at Hythe and used for the five day journey to Australia (during which the passengers stayed each night in a luxury hotel en route. . .) I found it quite fascinating. Even as the flying boats superceded travel by sea which took three or four weeks to Australia, so they in turn were overtaken by the jets which did the same journey in only hours, and carried many more passengers.

The Flight Engineer was very interesting on the subject of his wartime service. The seaplanes were well armed, but their vulnerable surface was underneath – which they protected by going down low over the water when chased, so that attackers could not get below them. In fact their gunners did so well against attacks from

Southampton was one of eight ports which was designated for this trade, which lasted roughly until the 16th century. Later the Wool House was used as a prison for French and Spanish captives. Now it has become Southampton's Maritime Museum, and is beautifully restored. There is a wonderful beamed roof of chestnut in the upper chamber which houses models of the *Queen Mary, Andes, Capetown Castle, Normandie, Stella* and other ships connected with the port. Also there I saw *Miss Britain III* (the actual boat) in which Hubert Scott-Paine broke the water speed record in Southampton Water in 1933, when he did 100.132 m.p.h. Mr. Scott-Paine had gone from Supermarine at Woolston to Hythe, where he started the British Power Boat Company, and subsequently he developed the 70 feet M.T.B. and M.G.B. craft which were of such value in the war –

On Itchen Ferry Hard, 1954, — the "Wonder" built by Dan Hatcher in 1860.

Southampton. High Street. The National Provincial Bank is on left, built 1833.

Courtesy H.E. Spencer

the Luftwaffe that the Germans nicknamed the flying boat "the Fliegende Stachelschwein"—the Flying Porcupine. he also said that it was very cold; the pilot and his second in command had the two seats with a view—even if it was only water and clouds which they saw, but the engineer was back behind them watching the instruments and dials.

I am sure small boys must have a terrific time at this exhibition. There are some twenty-six aircraft companies described, including the Supermarine Works where R. J. Mitchell designed the Schneider Trophy winning aircraft S6B, and the legendary Spitfire. This factory had been used to build flying boats since 1913, when it was owned by Noel Pemberton Billing and managed by the red headed Hubert Scott Paine.

Under the huge wing of the Sandringham is a Spitfire, and it is easy to see how a pilot inserting himself into the tiny cockpit must have felt that he had become a bird, and how very manoeuvrable these machines were. The pilots said that the Spitfires practically flew themselves. The first prototype made its test flight from Eastleigh in 1936, and Reginald Mitchell died in June 1937 when he was only forty-two, so he did not live to see how The Spitfires and Hurricanes saved us in the Battle of Britain. Test Pilot Jeffrey Quill lived at Bursledon—at River Barn in Salterns Lane, for some time, and we would watch him doing acrobatics overhead. He is now President of the Spitfire Society, founded in 1984, with members from many countries, men who had flown Spitfires, or had been connected with them.

Across the Itchen Bridge is what remains of the settlement at Itchen Ferry, badly bombed in the war, as it was right beside the Supermarine factory.

Before the present bridge, and even before the floating bridge service, early worshippers had a hazardous time getting across to St. Mary's in small boats which landed them at Crosshouse on the Southampton side of the river. Eventually a chapel was built at Pear Tree Green. There is a memorial stone in the churchyard to Richard Parker of Itchen Ferry, around whom was centred one of the most bizarre stores of the sea. He left Southampton over a hundred years ago, as a ship's boy aged seventeen, in a yacht named the *Mignonette*, bound for Australia. The yacht foundered, and the resultant tragedy is revealed in A.W.B. Simpson's book *Cannibalism And The Common Law*. The case attracted tremendous interest at the time, and it was argued from every angle by eminent counsel. There was a great deal of sympathy for the men who found themselves in such a desperate plight, and had to decide whether they all would die, or one be sacrificed so that the others might have a chance of survival.

Itchen Ferry gave its name to a type of small fishing boat. There has been some correspondence lately in regard to the amount of "shoulder" there was in the original design. (For non-boating readers assume that the bow is the head, and you will realise where the hull swells out is the shoulder). One of the contributors to this was a frequenter of Deacons Yard in the thirties, whom I remember as a dashing naval commander who wore a monocle and—on occasions—a boat cloak lined with scarlet. On a very wet regatta day recently I was accosted by a figure in a yellow oilskin suit and sou'wester, who said "Don't you remember me?" . . . After peering at the small amount of face which was visible I did—after fifty years—recognise the twinkle in the eye.

On the eastern side of Southampton I must mention Owen Farwell who was born at Sholing in 1906, and who in his travels around the world has accumulated a lot of interesting tales. He joined the Royal Mail Company at the age of sixteen, sailing between Europe and North and South America. Between whiles he went in yachts, and told me about the schooner *Elfay* which he said was the largest ever built purely for racing. She was a product of the famous firm of Herreshoff, of Bristol, Rhode Island, and was about 110 feet long with 32 feet beam and 19 feet draft. One of the early owners renamed her *Katoura*, and this man's daughter was lost overboard on a voyage from the West Indies to New York. He was so grieved that the yacht was laid up, and was rescued by Mr. W. G. Jameson of the Irish Whiskey firm after about four years, by which time it was very neglected and the ship-keeper had cut a hole in the foredeck to make an outlet for his stove. . . . Mr. Jameson was Sailing Master for King Edward VII and he sent a crew to America to collect the vessel. After Captain Charlie Toms had got her ready for sea the Americans suddenly realised that they were letting an exceptional yacht go abroad. Captain Toms could see objections piling up, so he announced that he was going out to swing the compass — and as soon as he was clear of the coast he kept going — eastwards. Mr. Jameson renamed the yacht *Magdalene*.

Magdalene was a lovely yacht, and Owen said that King George V in Cowes Week, liked to take her for a sail round the Nab Tower and back, just to get the feel of the ship.

One day in about 1925 they came out of Plymouth with the wind off the land and saw the steam yacht *Sapphire*, (which was one of the large steam yachts of the period), coming up channel. The wind freshened, *Magdalene* began moving fast, and those on board saw that the fires on *Sapphire* were being raked to improve her speed. Owen said "We got to Cowes and had all the sails down and the covers on them before *Sapphire* came in, and in the pubs at Cowes that night the talk was all about what we did to the steamer". . . . One point which struck him about her performance on that occasion was that when they came in through the Needles and the tide was running strongly against them, the ship trembled just as though she had an engine running. *Magdalene* was later sold to a Greek, and had yet another name-change, to *Lou Kiani*.

About two years after Owen Farwell told me about the *Elfay*, I had a visit from an elderly lady, Mrs. Norman, who had lived in Old Bursledon as a small girl, until her mother Mrs. Wheeler, a widow married a sailor and they moved to Southampton. The step-

A Sailor's wedding party outside the Vine Inn, Old Bursledon, early 1900's.   *Courtesy Mrs. G. Norman*

father, named Stephens, left the navy to crew on the large yachts of those days. Mrs. Norman recalled seeing Sir Tom Sopwith, who later owned the *Endeavour I* and *II* when he came to their house, and she also said that her stepfather went to America on a liner from Southampton "to bring back a yacht named *Elfay*. . . .' It is strange how once you have heard a name it turns up again quite unexpectedly.

Owen always says how lucky he has been in his life, but I suspect that his drive and enthusiasm had a great deal to do with it. As a lad he went to Switzerland and worked in hotels to improve his French and German, and this came in very useful later, on the Atlantic liners carrying emigrants from Eastern Europe to America, since he was able to act as interpreter for them.

He married and settled at Sholing again until the Second World

War when he went into the Royal Artillery, and was in Singapore when the Japanese took over. Here his experience with boats came in. He and some friends found an old gaff ketch and got it ready under cover of darkness, so that 180 men were able to sail away in it. They went up the Campar River in Sumatra and through thick jungle to Padang, living on what they could find. Then their luck ran out. They were taken prisoner, worked on the Sumatra railway, and were almost starved to death. After the war, Owen was invalided out as C.4. whereas he had been A.1. when he joined up. However, in time he recovered, got a job in Southampton Docks, and built a bungalow on a hillside at Bursledon, where he planted a garden of specimen trees and shrubs. Here he and his wife frequently had the Man of the Trees, Richard St. Barbe Baker, as a visitor. Sadly his wife Phyllis died, and when the Royal Hospital at Chelsea offered him a berth he accepted it.

Many shipbuilding firms have operated from Southampton's Itchen frontage over the years, with a considerable output of paddle steamers, floating bridges, tugs, steamships, and of course yachts. George Parson's grandson John Rubie owned the Crosshouse Yard from 1824, moving there from Warsash. The Northam Ironworks launched the P & O Company's *Hindostan* (253 feet) in 1869, and by 1892 had produced twenty-seven luxury steam yachts under the name of Summers and Day, and subsequently Summers and Payne. Thomas Chamberlayne had his own private yard where he rebuilt his own yacht *Arrow*, and this site was amalgamated with that of J. G. Fay who had been established since 1870—to form Camper and Nicholson's yard in 1912. There were many other small builders, Andrews, Ransom, Dan Hatcher. Camper and Nicholson's *Philante* was the largest diesel yacht built in the U.K. in her time, and is now the Norwegian Royal Yacht *Norge*. From here also came *Shamrock V* in the thirties. This has given the name to Shamrock Quay which commemorates the famous "J" class yacht, and is a marine trade centre with shops, chandlery, yacht brokers, and marina berths afloat.

Calling in at Shamrock Quay on a hot afternoon in mid July 1987, to see if the resident Diver had succeeded in finding a pair of spectacles dropped into the water off the marina on the previous day (and he had. . .) there was a great excitement to watch the lovely old schooner *Altair* being moved across to the launching site with the aid of a crane and a giant trolley. She was built by Fife and Son on the Clyde in 1931 and is 160 tons, 108 feet long. The original owner sailed her in the Solent, and now she has been fully restored, is going to Harry Spencer at Cowes for new masts and rigging, and in due course will be off to the Mediterranean.

One of the well known professional skippers who raced *Shamrock*, the schooner *Westward*, and others was Captain Alfred Diaper who died in 1950 aged seventy-eight. He is said to have won

"Velsheda" in the Ocean Dock at Southampton.   Photo David Dunn

more King's Cups than any other professional yacht-master.

On the east bank of the Itchen the Rampart yard at Bitterne Manor was for three generations in the Desty family, beginning with George Desty (1920), followed by his son Horace and daughter Doris, and in the years leading up to the second World War building very good twin-screw cruisers of wood. This traditional method they maintained regardless of the glass-fibre innovations. A number of their boats took part in the evacuation of troops from Dunkirk, and more were used for inshore coastal patrol work. The three sons of Horace took over the Warsash Yard (site of George Parsons activities) in 1985, and now operate from there as Victoria Rampart, with a new partner.

"Altair" on her way to launching at Shamrock Quay, Southampton. 1987.

Nearer the mouth of the Itchen, below the bridge at Woolston, is Vosper Thornycroft, where ships for our own and foreign navies have been built for many years. It was formerly J.I. Thornycroft, and before that was the yard of Oswald Mordaunt who went in for large iron sailing vessels. An elderly man whose father had been at the Oswald Mordaunt yard, told me that ironworkers who came from the north caused the failure of this business through restrictive practices. When they had earned sufficient for their needs they downed tools and stayed away, thus preventing the completion of ships within their time limit.

Vosper Thornycroft's Northam base bas been sold to the Hunting Group, and in consequence the 212 feet luxury yacht *Shemara* which formerly belonged to Sir Bernard and Lady Docker, has been moved down to the dock at the Ocean Village. It is the first move the ship has made in several years, but it looks in very good condition, well maintained, and all the tourists walk along the quay and gaze at it. In the days of the Dockers everything on board was reputed to be gold-plated. . . . Certainly no expense was spared— on the after deck are no less than six other craft, all neatly stowed.

When Thomas Oswald moved from Sunderland and opened his shipyard at Woolston he lived for a time at New Place House. This had been built in about 1800 on two acres of land at the junction of London Road and Bedford Place, and was said to be one of the principal mansions in the neighbourhood, having three storeys and ten bedrooms. On this site from 1893 until it was bombed in 1940 stood the town's first purpose built Public Library, later to be incorporated in the Civic Centre.

TITCHFIELD

If you follow the Solent Way footpath from Warsash eastwards, passing below the Navigation School grounds, you have a splendid view of yachts sailing in and out of the Hamble river, and go through land which is now a nature reserve. Here you may see a variety of birds, and some rare plants among the shingle. Eventually you will come to the tiny harbour, Titchfield (or Meon) Haven, which is at the mouth of the River Meon. Before access was blocked to this river by an embankment—reputedly at the instigation of a fifteenth century Earl of Southampton—barges and small boats could travel two miles inland to the little town of Titchfield, which in past times was a very busy place.

So, although it is little more than a village now, Tichfield has a very illustrious past, and it was interesting to see in the television film of the Heritage Museum in Leningrad, with commentary by Peter Ustinov, reference made to the massive dinner service ordered from England by Catherine the Great—each piece of which had a different scene on it—and the one which was shown was of Titchfield.

In contrast to the ornate tomb of the Earls, there is a simple stained glass memorial inset in the west window, to three sisters—the Misses Agnes, Edith and Mabel Hewitt, whose family had lived at Great Posbrook for 300 years, and who themselves lived at Bridge House in Titchfield for most of their lives. Miss Agnes was a pioneer woman farmer for fifty years, at Little Posbrook, Hollam, and Meon. Miss Edith was a well known grower of flowers and strawberries, and Miss Mabel was choirmistress at St. Peter's for nearly forty years. The Bishop of Salisbury (Dr. W. L. Anderson) unveiled the memorial, and described them as "three ladies who for more than half a century by their goodness and kindness enriched the life of the village". The designer, Francis Skeat, has depicted their activities—a man ploughing, strawberries and flowers, and Miss Mabel's collie together with the Hewitt crest.

A friend of mine, who was one of the Godfrey sisters of Locks Farm at Locks Heath (now an Abbeyfield House), remembers when her grand-parents had "Fernhills" the farmhouse beside the great Barn at Titchfield. She and her brother and sisters would walk across country from Locks Heath—all open fields then—to visit, and the Barn made a splendid place in which to play. What a history—a Queen's horses, Shakespeare's plays, and some five centuries of harvests gathered in.

There were many Flemish and Huguenot settlers in Titchfield, which fact is reflected in the local surnames. Some of the shops in the square extend back quite a way towards what would have been a busy river frontage in days long ago. There are some picturesque houses in South Street, and up on the hill to the west of the town is St. Margaret's Priory which was built by the Earls of Southampton

Titchfield Haven (Meon) 1934.

Titchfield. The ancient Barn — which Shakespeare knew.

as a dower house.

Apart from the river valley, the land between Titchfield and the Solent is fairly level, and is mainly used for market gardening. Some years back a family named Edwards had one of the farms, and a daughter, Pat told me that she remembered the Coward parents coming to a holiday cottage there, with their young son. Pat was one of the little local girls persuaded to act in a tragedy which Noel had written, and she said that he was furious when they forgot their lines and giggled—and he hit one of them on the head with a spade.

. . .

Pat farmed for most of her adult life, in Devon, and then lived in a lovely old thatched house Clyst Hayes, at Hele, which is about seven miles north of Exeter. When I stayed there I was very careful of my little Cavalier King Charles—never feeling quite sure that Pat's two Great Danes, Honey and Holly, would not mistake her for a rabbit, or something small to be chased. Clyst Hayes featured in several "Beautiful Devonshire" calendars, as an outstanding example of thatch.

Eventually Pat decided to come back to the Hampshire coast for her remaining years, and we all scoured the neighbourhood for her, because no "ordinary" house would do. We had no success, but the agents found the 13th century Crabthorne Farm House, tucked away in a lane off Old Street at Hill Head—which is the next place along from Titchfield Haven. There was a Granary on staddle stones, and a willow tree which is mentioned in Domesday, and green fields surrounded it all. Pat mowed the grass in the orchard, and soon had the garden looking beautiful, and she had several happy years before she was found dead one morning amongst her flowers—the kind of end I know she would have wished. Since then, although the house is still in its oasis, the fields have been covered with "little boxes". I am glad she did not see this, and that the country lasted for her.

The Edwards family had also lived at Segensworth Farm (now Segensworth House and no longer a farm) with a garden sloping down to the River Meon, not far from the Abbey ruins, and when I took Pat to see her old home, at the invitation of the owners, after she had been settled in at Crabthorne, she was delighted to find that a brick patch made by her mother years ago, was still there. The garden looked particularly lovely that spring day, with daffodils in the grassy banks which sloped to the Meon River.

I look back at Pat with great affection. She was a good English countrywoman, an outdoor person, very knowledgeable about the land, animals, plants and all the basic things. She had a stong sense of family, and to the end kept all her brothers and sisters in touch by air mail letters to all parts of the world where they had settled. When their friends came to England they stayed with Pat, and she was the centre of a wide circle of people from overseas.

In days gone by, when women needed money to eke out their husbands' meagre wages, many women from Titchfield went gathering shell-fish on Meon Shore. One of these—she was known as the "Winkle Queen" was Mrs. Violet Elms, who cycled to the beach on most days, and sometimes in the very early morning—according to the tide—and later sold her catch to the local people and to a Fareham fishmonger.

The Meon shore is part of my childhood—a beach hut and bathing and picnics, the marsh with high reeds, and trees shaped by the prevailing salty wind. There was a serious threat to the land between Warsash and Meon at one time, by a refinery project which would have made another Fawley on our side of Southampton Water, but luckily there was a great protest, and the scheme was dropped.

Now the estuary of the Meon is a Nature Reserve—lagoons were dredged out to encourage migrating birds, and a warden appointed to conduct bird-watchers. In the winter, well wrapped people with binoculars can be seen propped against walls and gates on the edge of the marsh. It really is a beautiful valley, and there is a footpath all the way to Titchfield.

The coast road from Titchfield Haven climbs to Hill Head village where the Osborne View Hotel looks across to the Isle of Wight, and then on to Lee on the Solent. At the top of a little chine where the lane suddenly turns inland, is a restaurant named the Swordfish which also has a good look-out. Along to the right is the airfield of H.M.S. *Daedalus* where warning notices tell you to beware of low flying aircraft. I always feel that these notices are on a par with "Beware of Subsidences" on roads in the Dukeries, and "Beware of Falling Rocks" in other parts of the country. What can you do to protect yourself? Nothing. . . .

Lee on the Solent is most adequately covered by a book in this series. I would only add that it is a quiet country seaside town, with cliff walks on grass, and some nice little shops in the main street which is one back from the front. Lee has changed little in fifty years, and has none of the nasty characteristics of "tripper" resorts. The most untoward happening which I can remember in a long aquaintanceship, is the afternoon in 1932 when the pier ballroom caught fire and was completely destroyed. My very first visit to Lee on the Solent was by train . . . which ran along from the Browndown direction, and ended by the pier.

It is aptly named, for it is indeed a lee shore and extremely shallow. One evening a distraught yachtsman appeared at my cottage—having sailed in too close, with the wind blowing in-shore. I telephoned our Yard Foreman and he took some men over there, but they could do nothing except take off the portable gear. The vessel was firmly fast and could not be moved before breaking up in the gale.

Eastwards again is Stokes Bay, and Alverstoke, where there is a simply splendid crescent of beautifully maintained white houses, just one road back from the shore. It is quite startling to find such an architectural creation so unexpectedly. At one end is the Anglesey Hotel, with a good restaurant, and also bar food. The crescent was built in the eighteen twenties, and was intended by the promoter, Lord Anglesey, to be the nucleus of a smart watering place. Also in the neighbourhood is another road of smaller houses named Little Anglesey.

Haslar Royal Navy Hospital is a short distance onwards, and the wall between the hospital and the water is a splendid viewpoint from which to see ships going in and out of Portsmouth Harbour entrance. The Royal Navy Submarine Museum is in this area too, and H.M. Submarine *Alliance* is open to view, also the Navy's first submarine *Holland*. The way from Gosport Ferry is signposted via Haslar Bridge—the old wooden construction which was there originally being referred to by the medical staff as "Pneumonia Bridge" for obvious reasons.

To yachtsmen the most interesting place at Gosport will probably be the world renowned yard of Camper and Nicholson. Here I saw the launching of the "J" class *Endeavour II* in the thirties, and in 1985 the assembly of ocean-going yachts which were about to set off on the Whitbread Round the World Race. Amongst them was *Drum* whose crew were extremely lucky to be rescued after the keel came adrift and the yacht capsized, only a short time before. Thanks to the staff at Moody's Yard at Swanwick, the keel was refitted in time for *Drum* to get to Gosport for the start, and in May 1986 she arrived back at Gosport after her long sail.

PORTSMOUTH HARBOUR

The early colonists who came in from the sea were looking for a sheltered and fertile land in which to settle, and therefore, they ignored the flat exposed Portsea Island site and continued on up the harbour and into Fareham Creek. The shallowness did not deter them because their boats were very small, and they could travel past the spot where the little Wallington river now comes up against the huge gyratory system of roads, with the viaduct overhead. Here also was the end of the track which came off Portsdown. These Jutish people could have brought little with them, but they became well established in the Meon Valley area, and a Jutish burial ground was unearthed near Droxford when the railway was being constructed.

The Romans were the next invaders and they built Portchester as a fort. Henry I added the Norman keep and founded an Augustinian Priory, the chapel of which is now Portchester Church, with splendid Norman work in it. Sir Walter Besant in "The Holy Rose" described the plight of French prisoners of war who were kept in the castle, the remains of which, with the church within its walls, and a few nice cottages outside, have become hemmed in by much modern housing and a very busy motorway — where once were flat fields stretching inland to the slopes of Portsdown Hill.

Fareham too has grown tremendously in recent years, but you can still visualise the little Georgian town it was, with the High Street, the parish church of St. Peter and St. Paul, the old inn The Red Lion and the creekside. Westwards in those days the road quickly became country, past Bishopswood (where the Bishop of Portsmouth lives), Blackbrook House (now a maternity home) and on to Titchfield. Overlooking Fareham Creek is what remains of Cams Hall.

With such a lovely site it seemed a great pity that the house was allowed to fall into its present state, but recently it was reported that an option has been secured to develop the 150 acre site and restore the mansion, which is described as Grade II listed, 18th century, and "shored up with scaffolding", also that the listed farm

Portchester High Street, Castle approach. 1950.   Photo Leslie Smith

Fareham High Street, about 1950.

Photo Leslie Smith

Fareham Creek, about 1950.

buildings are proposed as the core of an office campus.

There are many books giving the detailed history of Portsmouth and its association with Charles Dickens, Lord Nelson, Samuel Pepys, and many other famous people. For visitors many of the interesting places are near the water, so it is easy to view them. Old Portsmouth itself is a fascinating place in which to wander, with houses restored, the great variety of shipping, the Keppel's Head, and the wall tablet commemorating the arrival of Catharine of Braganza to marry Charles II – to name a few which particularly appeal to me. The Round Tower was part of Portsmouth's first permanent defence, and provides a vantage point for the harbour entrance. There are boat trips from Portsmouth Hard and also from the Clarence Esplanade, and in the summer one can go out to the Spithead Fort.

Other principal objectives are –

H.M.S. *Victory* and the Royal Naval Museum – entrance main Dockyard Gate, and also here the *Mary Rose* and the exhibition of items recovered from the ship.

The Royal Marines Museum at Eastney

The D-Day Museum near Southsea Castle. This was opened in 1984 and has the "Overlord" embroidery telling the story of the invasion. There is an award-winning audio-visual film in English, French and German, which is extremely realistic, and brings back all the war-time days if you happen to be old enough to remember them. This is a splendid exhibition.

H.M.S. *Foudroyant* which has been afloat in Portsmouth Harbour for a long time, has now followed in *Warrior's* wake to Hartlepool, for restoration.

In the middle of June 1987, H.M.S. *Warrior* – the Victorian iron-clad battleship, returned home, and I was delighted to be taken out to see her on arrival, with two tugs, south of the Nab Tower, on the day previous to her triumphal entry into Portsmouth Harbour.

Her sleek black hull, three masts and rigging, and Jack

Portsmouth Harbour entrance, showing the Round Tower.

Portsmouth. Old boathouse − outer camber (Point) about 1950.
Photo Leslie Smith

Whitehead's splendid figurehead in place, make her a beautiful sight to behold. As we left, a helicopter arrived, flying very low to take photographs, and on our way back to the Hamble the Beken launch from Cowes was streaking out towards the Nab, on the same errand. However, *Pipperi II* had been first on the scene, the owners, Frank and Ella Verrill, being very interested as they hail from Hartlepool and had seen *Warrior* in the course of her refit there. She is a great addition to the ships on view at the Naval Base.

Another Victorian candidate for restoration−at Gosport−is H.M.S. *Gannet* (1878), which in latter days, as a training ship was *Mercury* on the Hamble River for about fifty years, and known to the locals as *Noah's Ark*.

1895 was the 800th anniversary of the founding of the original church of St. Thomas a Becket on the site of what is now Portsmouth Cathedral. At the other end of the scale in size, is the church of St. Ann within the Naval Base, and the little chapel inside the grounds of Haslar Hospital. The roofless remains which can be seen on the starboard side as you enter Portsmouth Harbour are of the Garrison Church which was badly blitzed. The City's Guildhall has been rebuilt, but a video shown at the launching of a new book *The City At War* by Nigel Peake (Milestone Publications £9.95) clearly brought back memories of that time to the invited guests who inlcuded the Lord Mayor. Nigel Peake is special publications editor of the *Portsmouth News*, and was able to use the paper's wartime files backed by 264 photographs, many not previously published, by the former chief photographer, Vic Stewart. There were some lighter moments, one senior member of the News staff told me that he, as a small boy, was evacuated to the household of an Admiral's lady out in the country, and she regularly inspected the fingernails of her charges every morning, and included in their diet items he had not sampled before, such as tripe, and boiled beef and carrots. Children are notoriously suspicious of strange food, but that really sounded like a good menu for those days when the rations were so limited.

H.M.S. "Warrior" off the Nab, 15/6/87, on return from Hartlepool.

The next harbour along to the east from Portsmouth is Langstone, which has Hayling Island on the other side, and the village of Langstone (which was the port for Havant) at the top end. The old water and wind mill—now converted to a dwelling—is a much photographed building and there are two inns, the 15th century Royal Oak and The Ship.

There is a ferry across to Hayling Island from Eastney, or road access from Havant over a bridge. The tollbridge which was formerly here caused queues to form for miles in the summer, in pre-war days. The island is very flat, shaped like an inverted "T", which gives it a great length of sandy beach at the southern end, and makes it very popular. There is a golf course, and the Hayling Island Yacht Club is at Sandy Point.

As to history, William the Conqueror commanded French monks to build a church at South Hayling and a chapel at North Hayling—the latter still remaining with much of its twelfth century work intact. The original church at South Hayling was taken by the sea, but the present one is quite old. Domesday records that "a Saltern was in Hayling" and in later times there were five listed. For many years a certain amount of oyster dredging went on in Langstone and Chichester harbours on either side of Hayling.

Two of the boatyards have been there as long as I can remember—The Hayling Yacht Company Ltd., at Mill Rithe, and Sparkes. At the former Robert McKillian, Marine Surveyor, had an office long ago. He was an extremely nice man, but completely deaf from his war service (1914/18). He was very chatty, and most entertaining; some of his stories I have retold in previous books, with his permission, but of course he carried on without interruption because he didn't hear what other people were trying to say—unless you made a very determined effort, when he would cup his ear and watch your lips. He was one of our regular visitors at Deacons.

WOOTTON CREEK

This waterway is used by the car ferries from Portsmouth to Fishbourne, Isle of Wight, and then by yachts and all kinds of boats up as far as Wootton Bridge, where it is very short of water at low tide. Here is the Sloop Inn where one can sit and have a drink or a meal and look out at the scene. There is a frequent 'bus service between Ryde and Newport passing the door.

There are several holiday villages in the area, and little huts among trees in the wilder parts of the river bank away from the main road. I saw quite a lot of this one very hot day when I was in search of Jack Whitehead who is a dedicated wood carver and restorer of old ships' figureheads which he repairs and brings back

Wootton Creek.

into their original condition. That magnificent "Warrior" which stood inside the Dockyard Gate at Portsmouth for some time was the work of Jack and his colleague Norman Gaches, and it was later transported to Hartlepool and mounted on the ship

On this first attempt I was misdirected to the east bank of the river down Barge Lane, an unmade track which came to a dead end by a curious stone, which I suspect is handmade.... Plodding back to the bridge I found the way along the west bank, went through a holiday village with a pool in which people were splashing about, and others sitting under palm trees, and eventually arrived at my destination only to find that my quarry was away from home. All I could see was the back view of one of the figureheads in his workshop. After a rest on Mr. Whitehead's lawn by the water I walked back to the bridge, the 'bus to Ryde, the ex-London tube train along the pier, and *My Lady Patricia* ferry to Portsmouth. These new ferries are very fast, they do 30 knots when clear of harbour, and cross in 14 minutes, but you are asked to stay in your seat, and I really prefer the old ships *Southsea* and *Brading* where you can walk round during the crossing. In rough weather in the winter I should feel happier in one of the "old fashioned" boats.

Subsequently, Mr. Whitehead told me that he had been away in Newcastle for the start of the Tall Ships, and had spent that hot day helping a group of youngsters who were carving figureheads from blocks of polystyrene—and wishing himself back on the Creek. I asked how they did, and he smiled and said that the end product rather resembled the Easter Island figures. Well, who knows, there may be some budding figurehead carvers about—the only other local one at the moment seems to be someone at Emsworth. It is quite heavy work—the *Warrior* for instance weighs about 2 tons, and the block was composed of seventy planks of 12″ × 3″ Canadian yellow pine, glued together, the carving taking eighteen months.

Mr. Whitehead has a fine collection of photographs of the jobs he has done, and some of these have taken him to far away places. A particular beauty is the lady who adorns the *Falls of Clyde*, a Scottish built vessel which was the first four-masted fully rigged sailing ship to fly the Hawaiian flag. She was built in 1878 by Russell and Company, and was one of nine large sailing ships all named after Scottish waterfalls. The resoration was commissioned by the Bishop Museum of Honolulu, and the photograph shows the early stages of the figurehead, which was completed in 1974. This resulted in Mr. and Mrs. Whitehead spending three years in Hawaii, which they much enjoyed. I asked how the features of his sculptures were arrived at, and he said most of them just evolved, but he thought this particular one had a look of his daughter-in-law.

The two carvers, Jack and Norman, have created figureheads for the Sail Training ships *Sir Winston Churchill* and *Malcolm Miller*, a nine foot sperm whale for the converted Danish training schooner *Golden Cachalot*, a replacement coat of arms for Lord Nelson's *Victory*, and massive decorations for the stern of the Hudson Bay Company's replica of *Nonsuch* which is on display in Winnipeg. They made a figurehead of Capt. Scott, the Antarctic explorer, for a training schooner, and when the ship was sold later to the Sultan of Oman, they were asked to change it. The new name was *Youth of Oman*, and they carved the figure of a young turbanned Omani tribesman, with the name in Arabic. The list seems endless. . . .

The work on the figurehead of the famous clipper ship *Cutty Sark* (found in ten pieces in the bilges), led to considerably more. When Jack was asked if he could do some restoration on the figureheads in the collection he assumed there would be just a few—but by the time of the *Cutty Sark* Exhibition in June 1986 he had completed twenty-five . . . and I understand the collection totals well over a hundred.

In his workshop various battered ladies stand awaiting attention, one holding a little dog in the crook of her arm. A mermaid with a golden face was having extensive repairs—behind her shoulders much decayed wood has been removed, new will be grafted in, and her flowing tresses will be carved again. Jack said she belongs to a restaurateur who is retiring and taking his mermaid with him. He was offered an entirely new one, but was sentimentally determined to keep the original.

We sat outside in the autumn sun for a while, with the creek at high water, and then Mrs. Whitehead gave me tea in their sitting room, which might almost be aboard a yacht, since it has a beam across the ceiling and beautiful cupboards which came from the boat on which they lived when bringing up their sons, who of course sailed from an early age, with grandsons now following on in the same fashion. Mrs. Whitehead has done the painting of the finished figures, and has enjoyed travelling with her husband in the course of this fascinating career of his.

Of Wootton Bridge she regretted that the old tidal mill had been allowed to disappear, and I do remember that a friend of years ago said what an attractive scene it was with the mill and cottages and the backdrop of the downs behind in the distance. Alas I was too late to see it.

It is good to find that surviving figureheads are being restored,

Jack Whitehead working on early stages of the figurehead for the ''Falls of Clyde''.

because it is a very ancient tradition that a ship should have one. The Vikings had their dragons, and the early Egyptians went in for much decoration on their barges. The combination of weather and particularly salt water which ate into the paint, ensured that once a vessel was neglected the basic wood came under threat, and a great many were lost in this fashion. In days when wooden ships were built, a yard of any size had its own carver on the payroll. Some of the poor creatures which come into Jack's workshop are in a very sad state, but he takes care with them all, and, as he works, speculates on their history.

QUARR

Between the towns of Ryde and Wootton Bridge is Quarr Abbey, a comparatively modern establishment – but it is on the land which was occupied by the old Abbey of Quarr, which was founded in the reign of Henry I (1100 to 1135). He was a scholarly King who encouraged such centres of culture, and the Cistercians at Quarr formed a trio with the abbeys at Beaulieu and Netley, and suffered the same fate, in the time of the Tudors. The stone quarry at Binstead provided the material for the first abbey, and was also sent to the mainland to build those at Beaulieu and Netley. Mr. Whitehead tells me that it was worked until well into the last century, but the site is now covered with grass, trees, houses, and only names – Pitts Lane, Stonepitts etc. indicate its past use.

As a further connection with the mainland it is recorded that the monks of Quarr derived some of their income from the salt works at Lymington, by favour of Richard de Redvers who was then the Lord of the Isle of Wight. However, it seems clear that monks in those days earned any monies which were handed out to them – for example they were often ordered to build churches and chapels (as we have seen at Bursledon and Hayling Island). When one considers the enormous difficulty of transporting the stone for the

abbeys across the Solent in their primitive craft – no engines, only the wind and oars – and then manhandling it up the beach at Netley and from the Beaulieu River to site, it is quite amazing how they managed it all.

The present abbey is built of red brick, and the central tower can be seen above the trees from the road between Ryde and Wootton Bridge. On July 22nd, 1987 the anniversary of the suppression of the Cistercian Abbey in 1536 – there was a great gathering of Bishops and Abbots, for a solemn Mass of thanksgiving to celebrate the restoration of monastic life at Quarr, under the Benedictine rule.

LYMINGTON

This is the ferry departure port for Yarmouth, serving the western end of the Isle of Wight, and it is a busy town with nice individual shops – a rarity nowadays – and a street market on Saturdays. Church Street, High Street and St. Thomas's Street lie end to end, from the cobbled Quay Hill upwards towards the New Forest. Looking up Paterson (1824) to see what he had to say – his comment reads "Lymington is situated on the brow of a hill and commands a beautiful view of the English Channel (?) and the Isle of Wight; it has two convenient sets of baths, and sends two members to Parliament". In the foreword he says "where there are more than one inn they are inserted alphabetically in order to avoid partiality or preference". He was a careful man apparently. So Lymington had the Angel, Bugle, Hope and Anchor, Nag's Head and Red Lion. The place became a borough in about 1150. There was always a thriving salt industry, (5,000 tons recorded in 1804), and there was shipbuilding, plus iron smelting, the material for the latter coming from Hengistbury by barge. Celia Fiennes gave a very detailed description of the salt processing, which she inspected during her travels.

In modern times yachts and ferries have taken over the waterway which is very crowded. On the river bank is the Royal Lymington Yacht Club, while the Lymington Town Sailing Club uses one of the aforesaid Baths for their base. I am indebted to the Hon. Secretary for the information that there were originally two plunge baths and two tiled baths in the wings of the building, and that the premises are said to be haunted by the ghost of an old colonel who drowned in the plunge baths . . . . During the war it was used as an observation post by the Coastguards and was in a very neglected state, but the New Forest District Council rented the top room to the newly formed club in 1946, after which much of the refurbishing and repairing of the Bath House was done by volunteer members.

One of their tireless workers, and a great dinghy sailor was Bert Rand, who died suddenly at the age of sixty-nine, and to whom a memorial of special interest has been raised, by subscription from the 1200 club members, Bert's family and the local firm of Brookes and Gatehouse – who made the apparatus and defrayed some of the cost. It is an illuminated platform, housing wind-speed and direction indicators, together with a brass map showing the mudflats and buoys to be seen from its particular vantage point at the clubhouse.

One of the famous builders at Lymington (although he originally came from Hastings) was Thomas Inman, whose yacht *Arrow* raced round the Isle of Wight in 1851 against the schooner *America*, after which the Americas Cup series developed.

Another name linked with the town is Berthon. The Rev. Edward Lyon Berthon was Vicar of Romsey for 32 years, and he invented a collapsible lifeboat which could be carried aboard ship, taking up only a very small space – to quote "so that the problems

Lymington. Quay Hill. 1955.

Lymington. 1955.

of the most crowded ship carrying sufficient boats to accommodate every soul on board is solved by this ingenious invention". The original was 28 feet long, but it was only about 2 feet wide when shut, and it could carry 75 people. The craft I remember were very much smaller and intended for yachts' use. To produce these the Berthon Boat Company was founded in 1830, and it is still in business as Berthon International, with a marina next to their yard on the west bank of the river. In 1986 they launched the 35th *Arun* class R.N.L.I. Lifeboat, the first to be built at Lymington for twenty years, and have started work on another. Newhaven has recently received a new boat of the *Arun* class—they carry a crew of six or seven, are about 52 feet×17 feet and according to the Skipper could pick up seventy or eighty people if necessary.

Many owners go out on fishing trips from the western Solent harbours to the Needles area. One told me that he saw a circle of porpoises one day, swimming round and round about five deep, and gradually decreasing the size of the ring. When he got nearer he could see fish jumping in the centre. Then the outer members of the porpoise ring-a-roses dived beneath the surface, so that they prevented the shoal from taking evasive action, and inside this makeshift "bag" the mothers of the herd showed the babies how to deal with mackerel, by throwing them into the air and letting the youngsters catch them. This is a sight which few people have an opportunity to watch, and confirms what intelligent creatures they are.

Between the wars the X.O.D. class boats were very popular in the Solent—designed by Alfred Westmacott, many of them were built by Woodnutts of St. Helens. It is good to find that the Royal Lymington Yacht Club includes them in its racing programme, and I am told that there are now forty-two "X" class based at Lymington, although not all compete. Mr. Dover of the R.L.Y.C. tells me that the latest to be built is *Condor* which Lallows of Cowes have recently launched. Looking back to some yachting notes of May, 1936 it was interesting to see the following comment "As in the other yards on the Hamble, Deacons employees have been—and still are for that matter—very busy converting the X.O.D. boats so that they can carry the Bermuda rig in place of the gaff mainsail. The small yacht owner finds that in the "X"class he has a greater opportunity of success with the Bermudian rigging"...Mr. Stanley Steele who lived at Oslands on Swanwick Shore, (the house is now "The Old Ship") was a great supporter of the class, so he would have been gratified to find that the sail numbers have now progressed to 183.

Readers of Captain Marryat's *Children of the New Forest* will remember Jacob Armitage ventured into Lymington for essential shopping, keeping a good look out for Cromwell's soldiers.

William Allingham, the poet and literary personality, spent seven years at Lymington as a customs officer in the Old Customs House on The Quay. His verses "Up the Airy Mountain, Down the Rushy Glen" are perhaps the most widely known of his works, although not exactly with a New Forest flavour. The Victorian poet Coventry Patmore also lived here.

The church of St. Thomas juts out slightly into the street, and has a little cupola dating from 1670. Old ceiling bosses, preserved in a glass case, are painted in ancient colours, and the designs include a dolphin and one of three fish entwined, appropriate for a seaport. There are also some interesting memorials.

Adlard Coles and his wife lived in Bursledon for about thirty years and then he "retired" from group publishing in 1967 and moved to Lymington where he set up as the Nautical Publishing Company in partnership with his former rival in ocean racing, Commander Errol Bruce. Adlard was a remarkable man, unassuming yet outstandingly successful in the toughest conditions at sea—Yachtsman of the Year in 1957, and winner of many awards. He was the author of some twenty-six books to the date of his autobiography which was published in 1981. He was painstakingly careful

"X" Class "Helena" 1949.

The trunk containing all her possessions was too large to go into the cabin, and took up most of the cockpit—a story which she says she will never live down. She continued to accompany him on cruises and support him until they reached their Golden Wedding and beyond. They did much sailing in the Baltic and off the coasts of France and Ireland, and he constantly refers to her "good eyesight" which was a great help in recognising lights and marks.

While being essentially a book on cruising and racing there is the underlying thread of the happiness shared by these two people in a lifetime partnership, and he touchingly ends the book "And of all my good fortune, the greatest is my wife Mamie, who came on our sailing honeymoon in *Annette*, with her big trunk, fifty-six years ago".

In three programmes which appeared on B.B.C. television recently, entitled "After Adlard Coles" Paul Heiney sailed around the Solent in *Grace O'Malley* visiting some of the ports mentioned in *Creeks and Harbours of the Solent* which is a nautical guide updated many times since it first appeared in the thirties, and Mrs. Coles was shown with him in the introduction to each programme.

of detail in the compilation of his pilot books and manuals on sailing practice. When he published my first book he dinned into me this attention to detail, and the men who crewed for him said that he insisted on extremely close attention to rigging etc., very wisely of course because one weak link can prove fatal to safety in bad weather.

I enjoyed his autobiography *Sailing Years*, particularly in the early chapters where he described a cruise to the Baltic and the Frisian Islands, where the action of Erskine Childer's *Riddle of the Sands* took place. Throughout his book he includes little pieces about his wife Mamie, who started off with him on their honeymoon on the tiny *Annette* only 26 feet 6 inches overall and 19 feet 2 inches on the waterline—not everyone's idea of a honeymoon.

THE BEAULIEU RIVER

This river has preserved the beautiful aspect which its name implies. Lord Montagu's Harbour Master is responsible for the control of the moorings, and it is not over-crowded. The Estate, of which the river forms part, is designated an area of outstanding natural beauty, and has become a major tourist attraction in as much as there is a great deal to see at Beaulieu itself.

Visitors may see the Abbey ruins, the Refectory (which is now the Parish Church), the Great Gatehouse (now Palace House), the Domus (which houses an exhibition of the time of King John and the monastic period), the National Motor Museum which tells the

Beaulieu Abbey — arcading.   Photo Leslie Smith

story of motoring from 1894, and alongside it a Motorcycle Museum with many working models. There is a Model Railway, and there is a Motorail which tours the grounds—really a great deal to interest everyone.

Beaulieu village is quite small and in the midst of it is the Montagu Arms Hotel, which in addition to providing accommodation and a restaurant, has the wine bar alongside which is convenient for lunches.

About two miles down river is Bucklers Hard. This hamlet was built in 1724 by John, Duke of Montagu, as part of a scheme to import sugar from the West Indies. In 1742 William Wyatt whose family had owned a shipbuilding yard at Bursledon, moved to Bucklers Hard, and set up his own yard, being succeeded eventually by Henry Adams who lived in the Master Builder's House—which is now the hotel. This is at the river end of the two rows of cottages which form the village. The yard was named *Agamemnon* after Lord Nelson's favourite ship which was launched here in 1781, and had a varied service, in many battles, finally sinking in the River Plate in 1808 while seeking shelter in stormy weather.

Some of the cottages are now used for exhibition purposes and there is a Maritime Museum which was opened by Lord Mountbatten in 1965, one of the exhibits being a model of the 40 gun *Beaulieu*. There is also an Information Office, and the Harbour Master's Office (the latter, telephone Bucklers Hard 200).

In summer the Blue Funnel boats run cruises from Southampton to the Beaulieu River.

My first memory of it goes back to the nineteen twenties when a yacht *Sigurd* was being delivered from the Hamble and I was taken along too. We landed somewhere at Exbury and walked through the woods to the main road, where we were collected by car. Now I visit Exbury gardens every year without fail, and after passing through successive "stage sets" of magnificent flowers come down to the river, and look out across the sedge between gnarled oaktrees. The gardens were the creation of Mr. Lionel de Rothschild who bought the estate in 1919, and in the period between the two great wars he employed many men on the project. There was even a little train to carry the rocks which now make the waterfalls and other features. The large trees which were already growing at Exbury provided shelter for the rhododendrons and azaleas, and it really is a most wonderful garden, and a "must" for every gardener and plantsman and anyone who loves flowers. I take all my visitors and watch their stunned appreciation. It is open every day from about March 8th to July 14th, according to the season. The camellias, magnolias and bulbs are the first to bloom.

In one of the glades is a small memorial to the man who made such a contribution to beauty. Appreciative visitors include H.M. The Queen, H.M. The Queen Mother, H.R.H. The Prince of Wales as well as thousands of other people. In fact, Exbury's great popularity means that you can no longer park on the grass beside the house (as one did in the beginning), and walk immediately into fairyland, but must go into a "proper" park. However, wheelchairs are available, there is a refreshment room, and a section where plants are sold. If you can go in the morning—it opens at 10.00 a.m. in the season—that is the time to see it at its best. You might also catch a glimpse of Mr. Edmund de Rothschild and his gardener Doug Betteridge. They continue the work of plant hybridising which has made the name of Exbury famous and for which first class awards are deservedly won at major shows.

The good news about Exbury is that the house may be lived in again. In 1942 it was taken over by The Admiralty at 48 hours notice, and Mr. Edmund de Rothschild has lived at Inchmery House, which is nearer the Solent, for some years.

Beaulieu Village, about 1950.

Bucklers Hard cottages, about 1953.

Everyone should drive carefully on the Forest roads, for as well as the ever present risk to ponies and their foals (and sadly many of them are killed each year), you may come over a little rise to find a cow taking its rest in the middle of a narrow lane with deep ditches on either side. One day on the way to Exbury, down that lovely little lane lined with bluebells, a huge bird launched itself across the front of the car, on a level with the windscreen. By courtesy of my friend who was driving, it reached the opposite side intact. It was a peacock . . . I have seen peahens getting up onto walls, very clumsily, but never before have I seen a male bird behaving so recklessly. They are too slow and heavy for this kind of antic. Also in this area, you often see golden pheasants which stray from the gardens.

In the late forties and early fifties Elizabeth Goudge wrote several delightful novels which were set in this part of Hampshire – The Salt Marshes, Beaulieu, Bucklers Hard and round about – *The Herb of Grace*, and *The Heart Of The Family* to name two of them. There was of course, Nevil Shute's *Requiem For A Wren*. Bearing in mind the great success of his books with their splendid story-telling, Reg Calvert recalled the days when he and Nevil Norway were fellow draughtsmen, and the latter was extremely worried about his lack of success in that occupation, and concerned regarding his chances of making a living. This was before he had started on his writing career. In this book there is a great deal about the pre D-Day period when the Beaulieu River was one of the centres for landing craft and other preparations for the invasion of France. The Wren is sent to "Exbury Hall", and wanders down through the gardens – then tended by fifteen old men instead of fifty able bodied gardeners – to the river. As a description it has no equal, and of course, with this author there is a good plot and an original one.

Tommy Fox in his waterside garden at Bursledon in 1950, with Phyllis Woodford and Leslie Smith.

POSTSCRIPT TO THE VILLAGE

Inevitably after reading the Bursledon story in the *Hamble River* book, people came along with more items which they wished had been included. Mrs. Rose Martin said that her uncle had been a river pilot, and received a guinea for each of the sailing coasters he guided in. He lived somewhere at Lands End. Another item which may tie in with this, refers to a remark by Mr. W. G. Richards – that in the garden of the four cottages which stood on the site of "Tara" there was the base of what he believed was a look-out tower of some kind, which would have enabled the people living on the north facing side of the bank to look down-river southwards for expected craft.

Mr. Richards was one of the last tenants of this row, before demolition, occupying two of the cottages knocked together, and he made a delightful garden, with a pond, and masses of hydrangeas. In another lived Fred Goddard, a jobbing gardener and a very shy man — so much so, that if spoken to he would fix his gaze on some distant object, or on the ground and avoid looking at you as he replied. The third tenant was Tommy Fox, (an old friend of Francis Deacon to whom the cottages belonged) who found this riverside retreat an ideal place for his retirement. He always referred to it as "my hovel" which it probably was in comparison with the life-style he had enjoyed in his early days when he was in the company of Barney Barnato and the racing fraternity. Tommy and Fred were as dissimilar as any two people could be, but they lived very amicably as near neighbours, each respecting the others privacy.

The land which is now the recreation ground in Long Lane was formerly cultivated by Harry Corbin, who lived at Elmdale, the cottage at the junction of High Street and Lands End Road. His mother Mrs. Hunt had a sweetshop there, and in the strawberry season would wear a sunbonnet and ride on the cart taking the fruit to the station. Harry had a voice which could be heard several fields away and he was constantly "hushed" by his housekeeper — a nice little woman who looked after him following the death of his mother.

He also owned Dale and Woodbine cottages in High Street, and in the latter lived Neddy Biggs, for many years a porter at Bursledon Station. After the "elevation" of Stationmaster Tarrant to Netley (it was "elevation" because fast trains stopped there — which they didn't do at Bursledon), Neddy, together with Freddie Cook, managed Bursledon and its signalling and its maintenance, and kept the whole place spotless and trim. A bright fire burned in the waiting room/booking hall in the winter. In fact it was so welcoming that a certain elderly couple could often be found sitting one on either side of the fire — the wife saying somewhat apologetically to anyone who came through 'Well, it's such a pity to waste it'.

Two retired seafarers were at Dale Cottage within living memory. One was Captain James from the days of the sailing coasters, a good looking courteous man, who usually wore a peaked cap and navy blue reefer jacket, and pottered towards the river for his daily walk. He was a contemporary of Oliver Fox who lived with his sister Mrs. Hallett in Yew Tree Cottage, and had also been on the coasters.

The later occupant was Captain Leonard Evans, whose life at sea began when as a boy he accompanied his father — Captain W. Evans of Gosport, in the delivery of the 45 ton yawl *Godwit* (an 1894 Fife built boat) to Bombay, in 1902. At the age of seventy-two, in 1959, he was still at it, arriving in Bermuda with a 56 foot sloop the *Chicane;* after an Atlantic crossing which was beset with gales. Captain Evans wore a beret at an angle, and smoked a pipe, and he wore little gold earrings. He was a grave and dignified figure of a man.

In the nineteenth century Elm Lodge (Greyladyes) was owned by the High Sheriff of Hampshire, W. C. Humphrys, and in June 1985 the *Hampshire* magazine printed a most fascinating and detailed article, by his great-grand-daughter, of the wedding in 1870 of one of the daughters of the house. There were several pages giving particulars of the presents, the guests, what they wore and what they ate, the speeches they made and the poems they quoted. It was a delightful account. It seems there were five sisters, and I have always heard that the bungalow at the top of Station Hill was built for one of them who expressed a wish to have a place of her own. The cottage has a very pleasant look-out onto the river. There was a path from Elm Lodge around the park to St. Leonard's Church, passing through a piece of woodland which is now part of my garden. After reading about the wedding I was digging one day and turned over some earth in which something glinted. It was a tiny gold ring, with initials which appear to be "B. H." and I won-

Fancy Dress Dance, May 1919.

and it is reckoned to be of quite considerable age, since it was 5 feet underneath a two hundred year old tree. It is about 15 feet long by about 2 feet in diameter, carved and slotted, and it is at present in the Carron Farm Barn at Segensworth, Titchfield, for safe keeping.

One day in the church I encountered Mr. H. J. Fay, who knew it well in his boyhood, his grandfather John Harding having been the verger and gravedigger for years, and his cousin John Armstrong the organist and choirmaster at a later date. Mr. Fay subsequently brought me several old photographs, one of John Harding taken outside the cottage which was part of the row of four

der if it once belonged to Bertha, Beatrice, or Rosalind Blanche, those Victorian girls who lived in this village more than a hundred years ago.

A photograph which came to hand is of customers of the Vine Inn as they appeared at a fancy-dress dance in 1919. It included Mr. and Mrs. Tom Robertson who then lived at the Dolphin and had a coal yard there, Bill Spencer who lived at Primrose Cottage with his wife and eleven children, Mrs. White—mother of Eddy (Knocker) of Deacons Yard, and Mrs. Pratt who was wife of the chauffeur at Greyladyes and lived in the house which is now numbers 5 and 6 Greyladyes. it will be noted that five of the men are still in Army uniform.

Since the previous book was written the "Bursledon Beam" has come to light. It was found below the roots of a fallen oak in a garden near Badnam Creek, and luckily the owner realised its importance. The Marine History Society had it examined and removed,

Memorial to John Taylor, dated 1693, on north wall of Bursledon Church.

Interior of St. Leonard's Church at Bursledon, 1950. (Used for wedding in Howards' Way).

in Bursledon High Street where he lived. There is one of the choir of small boys with John Armstrong in their midst, and in the back row Colin Swift, architect of the meeting room which has so well merged into a niche alongside the church. There is a photograph of the choir men, posed in and beside one of those bulbous "charabancs" in which outings were made. There is a photograph of the old original graveyard, now a dark tunnel of yew and other trees, but then much more open and with even a palmtree beside the path. There is a group of strawberry pickers, the women in large hats and not in the sunbonnets which appear in many of the early pictures.

The grave-digger received frequent visits from the local undertaker, and after the immediate business was settled there would often be a chat about village affairs, in the course of which the small boy would overhear items which stuck in his memory.

One of these concerned "Lovely Emma" who had been sold by her husband at the Fox and Hounds. It seems that in her old age she could hardly walk because her toenails had grown to such a length. Presumably there were not any chiropodists then—or at least no one to whom she could call for help, which seems a sad state of neglect for a once beautiful woman. In those days there was no National Health Service, but the village had a Nursing Association to which most people contributed, and there was an annual fete to raise funds. This was usually held in the grounds of Ploverfield.

Another voice from the past was that of Chris Walker who taught at the school in Hamble Lane until 1947. She then had two years in Gibraltar and six in Tanganyika, married, was widowed, and now lives in Rochester. She asked about many of her old girls from the guide troop of which she was captain.

The first Bursledon Guides Company was started in 1925 by Miss Sheila Garton (later Mrs. Norris-Hill) and her sister Nancy (later Mrs. Trench) who ran the Brownies. They lived at Brixedon until they married, and the troop was then taken over by Miss Rosamund Oliver of Oak Hill. (This house is now the Crow's Nest Hotel). In 1935 she was succeeded by Chris Walker, who says that the guides met at St. Benet's Hall (in Greyladyes outbuildings) until the outbreak of war, then the house was taken over by the Royal Artillery. The guides then used a room over the stables at the Old Rectory, but after a weekend away, Chris found that this too had been commandeered by the Army, and she had great difficulty in retrieving their goods. Mr. Batchelor on Lowford Hill lent them a room over his large store. They had to give up meetings there because of the bombing, but they worked hard salvaging newspapers, which were sorted at Windhover (there was a house in what is now the middle of the roundabout), and they raised quite a lot of money towards various war charities.

Although only four miles from Southamptom, Old Bursledon is a very peaceful place, particularly in the daytime. The narrow lanes

Strawberry Pickers at Bursledon.

are in circles, some end in the marshes, and on fine summer evenings there are many motorists enquiring the way to either the Jolly Sailor or the Fox and Hounds Barn Restaurant, but in the morning quiet reigns again, the river views give endless pleasure, the yachts are reflected in the water, and the only sounds are the cries of the gulls, the jingle of rigging on metal masts, and the tannoy on the Moody Swanwick Marina requesting Mr. So-and-So to go to the nearest telephone.

There has been an increase in the number of sightseers at weekends since the filming ot the B.B.C. serial "Howard's Way", when many of the houses became the imaginary abodes of various characters. The producers sent us polite letters hoping that their activities would not inconvenience us, but personally I was interested in all the goings-on, and particularly the night filming when the huge lights made everything look like fairyland, and moths, disturbed, fluttered out of the trees. A wedding was filmed in the old Shipbuilders Church, but, beyond a little feminine curiosity to know which of the characters was the bride, no-one took much notice the participants and their vans of equipment are taken for granted, and the village goes about its business of daily living.

In September 1986 the last gap in the riverside path from Swanwick to Warsash on the east bank of the Hamble River was bridged, so it is now possible to walk this beautiful stretch again, after a lapse of some forty-five years. The final section was rebuilt by Community Service youngsters, and was completed by a "Willow Pattern" timber construction made by Technical Timber Services Ltd., of Romsey. It makes possible the round trip walk taking in Lower Swanwick, Warsash, the ferry across to Hamble, Satchell Lane, the footpath through the woods to Old Bursledon High Street, and then downhill to Swanwick—or the same thing in reverse.

And the other piece of good news is that there are now some otters in the region of the Swanwick Marina, so those fat grey mullet which used to weave about in the shallow warm water under my office window at Deacons will have to keep a sharp look out. . . .

Elm Lodge (later Greyladyes) Bursledon, as it was in 1906.
Courtesy H.J. Fay

1st Bursledon Company Girl Guides. 1934. Miss R. Oliver on right.
Courtesy Chris (Walker) Morgan

Looking across the river from Bursledon to Swanwick. No Marina.

Bursledon about 1910. Railway station on right. There is only one building on the "Elephant" site — the Boathouse.

Shore Road, Warsash.

Courtesy Mr. H. Fay

Bursledon 1884. This shows the river before the Railway Bridge was built.

ACKNOWLEDGEMENTS

My sincere thanks to all the people who have written, talked to me, and brought photographs for this book. Unfortunately with limited space it has only been possible to include a few, but in particular I would draw attention to the 1844 view of the river at Bursledon, before the Railway Bridge was built. How beautiful it was then . . .

Thanks must also go to Keith Beken for supplying the beautiful cover picture showing *'Velsheda'* and *'Astra'* racing in the Solent, another *'J'* class yacht *'Shamrock'* is also visible in the background.

Do you have the complete set of 'Down Memory Lane' on Old Hampshire?

1 THE CINEMAS OF PORTSMOUTH
A nostalgic look at the area's picture palaces of the past, including Gosport and Fareham. Also features many Stars of the Silver Screen. Ron Brown

2 ARE YOU BEING SERVED? A reminder of some of the shops and businesses that flourished in the Gosport of yesteryear, from grocers to undertakers. Ron Brown

3 'I REMEMBER WHEN IT WAS JUST FIELDS' THE STORY OF HAYLING ISLAND Including the Hayling Billy, early lifeboats and ferries, sailing days, holiday camps, and the shops and characters of the Island of yesteryear. Ron Brown

4 THE STORY OF LEE-ON-SOLENT
Although the watering spa of Lee-on-Solent has only really developed over the past one hundred years, it has lost much in that period: a pier, a railway, and an extremely unusual entertainment complex. Ron Brown

5 TRANSPORTS OF DELIGHT The history of, and stories about, Gosport's transport system, including horse coaches and trams, electric trains, railways, ferries, etc. Ron Brown

6 TIME GENTLEMEN PLEASE An historic pub crawl around the inns and taverns of old Gosport. Ron Brown

7 FAIRDAYS AND TRAMWAYS, THE STORY OF COSHAM Including the fair, Wymering Race Course, Alexandra Hospital and the famous Portsdown and Horndean Light Railway. Ron Brown

8 AT YOUR SERVICE A look at some of Gosport's essential services, including water, gas, electricity, police, fire brigade, education, workhouse, nursing and civic affairs. Ron Brown

9 THIS SPORTING LIFE Gosport's sporting past: football, cricket, bowls, model yachting, boxing, hunting etc. Ron Brown

10 THE 1906 GUIDEBOOK TO PORTSMOUTH AND SOUTHSEA
A nostalgic reminder of Portsmouth's great Edwardian past. If you had visited the city during 1906 you would have needed this Guide Ron Brown

11 THE WINDMILLS OF HAMPSHIRE
A fascinating study, profusely illustrated, of every windmill in the county spiced with many milling tales. Anthony Triggs

12 THE PORTSMOUTH EMPORIUM
A nostalgic journey around some of the traders, shops and businesses that flourished in the Portsmouth that has passed, from grocers to undertakers. Ron Brown

13 THE FAREHAM OF YESTERYEAR
A nostalgic reminder of Fareham past including: marketdays, the railway, transport, mills, trades and industries, shops and businesses, famous buildings, sport etc. Ron Brown

14 THE THEATRES OF PORTSMOUTH
Details the history of the Kings, the Theatre Royal and every other theatre in the city over the years. John Offord

15 THE HAMBLE RIVER And much about old Bursledon. The fascinating story of the river including early sailing days and many colourful local characters. Susannah Ritchie

16 SPRINGBOARD FOR OVERLORD
Hampshire's most memorable event during the Second World War was the departure of tens of thousands of Allied troops to France on D-Day June 6th, 1944. This book looks at the preparations for 'Operation Overlord' and the everyday lives of people in South Hampshire at the time. Anthony Kemp

17 THE PUBS OF PORTSMOUTH
Packs in over 1,000 pubs and 125 photographs Ron Brown

18 SOUTHAMPTON REMEMBERED
A photographic look at old Southampton with a brief history of the city. Maureen Burness

19 EASTLEIGH AN ILLUSTRATED HISTORY
An illustrated history of the town and its council from 1895 to recent times.

20 GO TO BLAZES
The fascinating history of fire-fighting in Portsmouth from the very earliest times, throughout two World Wars to today.